Woman Talk

Volume One

Woman Talk

Volume One

A Woman's Book of Quotes

Michèle Brown
&
Ann O'Connor

MACDONALD & CO
LONDON & SYDNEY

To our daughters

A Macdonald Book

First published in Great Britain in 1984
by Macdonald & Co (Publishers) Ltd
London & Sydney

ISBN 0-356-10231-9

British Library Cataloguing in Publication Data

Woman talk.
1. Women – Quotations, maxims, etc.
I. Brown, Michele II. O'Connor, Ann
305.4 PN6084.W6

Typeset, printed and bound in Great Britain by
Hazell Watson & Viney Limited
Member of the BPCC Group
Aylesbury, Bucks

Macdonald & Co (Publishers) Ltd
Maxwell House
74 Worship Street
London EC2A 2EN
A BPCC plc Company

ACKNOWLEDGEMENTS

In compiling this collection of quotations we have used material gathered from a vast variety of sources, ranging from newspaper articles, chance remarks heard on TV and elsewhere, magazine features, biographies. Among the books we have consulted are:

A Solitary Woman, Henrietta Sharpe (Constable); *The Memoirs of Sarah Bernhardt*, Ed. Sandy Lesberg (Peebles Press); *Just Barbara*, Barbara Woodhouse (Michael Joseph and Rainbird); *Amy Johnson*, Constance Babington Smith (White Lion); *Audacity to Believe*, Sheila Cassidy (Collins); *Virginia Woolf and Her World*, John Lehmann (Thames & Hudson); *Lilian Baylis: The Lady of the Old Vic*, Richard Findlater (Allen Lane); *Horatia Nelson*, Winifred Gerin (Oxford University Press); *Marie Stopes: A Biography*, Ruth Hall (André Deutsch); *Eminent Victorians*, Lytton Strachey (Chatto); *The Pelican Guide to English Literature* (Penguin); *The Talkies*, Richard Griffith (Dover Press); *Ellen Wilkinson*, Betty D. Vernon (Croom Helm); *Chanel*, Edmonde Charles-Roux (Jonathan Cape); *On Lies, Secrets and Silence*, Adrienne Rich (Virago); *The Female Eunuch*, Germaine Greer (Paladin); *Graffiti*, Nigel Rees (Unwin); *Miss Piggy's Guide to Life*, Muppet Press (Michael Joseph); *My Favourite Comedies in Music*, Victor Borge & Robert Sherman (Robson Books); *Off the Wall*, Rachel Bartlett (Proteus); *Now for the Good News*, Robert Dougall (Mowbrays); *Dylan Thomas*, Andrew Sinclair (Michael Joseph); *The Encyclopaedia of Insulting Behaviour* (Futura); *Beecham Stories*, Ed. Harold Atkins & Archie Newman (Robson Books); *The Bandsman's Daughter*, Irene Thomas (Macmillan); *Violets and Vinegar*, Jilly Cooper & Tom Hartman (Allen & Unwin); *The Complete Husband*, Gyles Brandreth (Sidgwick and Jackson); *Woman, Fancy or Free*, Nan Berger & Joan Maizels (Mills and Boon); *A Summer Bird-Cage*, Margaret Drabble (Weidenfeld & Nicolson); *Side Effects*,

Woody Allen (New English Library); *My Cousin Beatrix*, Ulla Hyde Parker.

Thanks to one and all.

APOLOGY

It has been our wish to give brief background information concerning the authors of all quotations used; sometimes, however, our efforts have been unsuccessful. We therefore extend our apologies to those whose words are attributed by name only.

CONTENTS

INTRODUCTION

This is not intended to be a book with a message. It has no axe to grind, except the all too obvious one (since almost every other book of quotations is dominated by the words and ideas of men) of redressing a long-overdue balance. If women do indeed hold up half the sky, as Chairman Mao was fond of telling the five hundred million or so of our sex in China, our aim has been simply to blow away the clouds and let the light shine from that portion supported by the rest of us.

Our hope was to present a balanced picture of women's ideas, aspirations, hopes, desires and frustrations throughout history. It has been a long and erratic path, littered with enticing by-ways along which we have wandered to spend many happy hours renewing old acquaintances and making new friends. On the way we have collected many fellow travellers – not all of them women. In trying to offer a full and rounded collection of quotations about and concerning women we have happily embraced husbands, fathers, brothers, lovers and other male admirers (as well as many vociferous adversaries).

Throughout, the entries are divided into fourteen sections each covering a specific theme or field of feminine experience. We have tried to provide consistent background information to each quotation, but we hope the reader will bear with us in those circumstances where this has been impossible.

While some may accuse us of dodging the current debate on the vigorous advancement of women's rights, we can only say in our defence that it was never our intention to focus on one specific area of feminine experience or interest. We have tried to compile a guidebook to be dipped into at leisure, not a bible to be studied with passionate intensity. Whatever enjoyment or insight the reader may gain from it is due entirely to the words of the person quoted. Our own enjoyment has come from bringing the two together.

Michèle Brown
Ann O'Connor

WOMEN ON WOMEN

LISA ALTHER (*b.* 1944)
American writer
In *Kinflicks*

There was nothing wrong with her that a vasectomy of the vocal chords wouldn't fix.

MAYA ANGELOU (*b.* 1928)
American writer

Most plain girls are virtuous because of the scarcity of opportunity to be otherwise.

ANON
In *New York World*, 1866
On Susan B. Anthony, American suffragette

Susan is lean, cadaverous and intellectual, with the proportions of a file and the voice of a hurdy-gurdy.

MARGOT ASQUITH (1865–1945)
British society hostess
In *Autobiography*, on Jennie Jerome Churchill

Had Lady Randolph Churchill been like her face, she could have governed the world.

GERTRUDE FRANKLIN ATHERTON (1857–1948)
American novelist
In *The Conqueror*

Women love the lie that saves their pride, but never an unflattering truth.

KATHERINE BATES (1859–1929)
American poet
Quoted in Klaus Lubber's *Emily Dickinson*

Emily Dickinson is the perfect flowering of a rare but

recognizable variety of the New England gentlewomen of the past – the lily-of-the-valley variety, virginal, sequestered, to the passing eye most delicate and demure, but ringing all the while spicy bells of derision and delight.

MARY RITTER BEARD (1876–1958)
American historian

The dogma of woman's complete historical subjection to man must be rated as one of the most fantastic myths ever created by the human mind.

ALIANA GIANINI BELOTTI
Italian feminist
In *Little Girls*, 1973

No woman, except for so-called 'deviants', seriously wishes to be male and have a penis. But most women would like to have the privileges and opportunities that go with it.

CONSTANCE BENNETT (1904–1965)
American actress
On Marilyn Monroe

There's a broad with her future behind her.

CHARLOTTE BRONTË (1816–1855)
British novelist
On her sister Anne

. . . hers was naturally a sensitive, reserved, and dejected nature; what she saw sank very deeply into her mind; it did her harm.

BRIGID BROPHY (*b.* 1929)
British writer
'Sayings of the Week' (*Observer*)

For every woman trying to free women there are probably two trying to restrict someone else's freedom.

MARY BULL
in Andrew Sinclair's *The Better Half*
On Susan B. Anthony, American suffragette

I have seen scarecrows that did credit to farmers' boys' ingenuity, but never one better calculated to scare all birds, beasts and human beings.

FANNY BURNEY (1752–1840)
British novelist and diarist
In *Fragments on Women*

Let no weak fears, no timid doubts, deter you from the exertion of your duty, according to the fullest sense of it that Nature has implanted in your mind. Though gentleness and modesty are the peculiar attributes of your sex, yet fortitude and firmness, when occasion demands them, are virtues as noble and as becoming in women as in men: the right line of conduct is the same for both sexes, though the manner in which it is pursued may somewhat vary, and be accommodated to the strength or weakness of the different parties.

LISA CALOGEROPOULOS
Mother of Maria Callas, former mistress of Aristotle Onassis

Why did he (Onassis) marry that Jackie? She is ugly, with horrible legs, the skin of a hen, fat in the wrong places, and eyes too far apart from one another. She's a big nothing.

MRS PATRICK CAMPBELL (1865–1940)
British actress
On a Broadway star (unidentified)

She's a great lady of the American stage. Her voice is so beautiful that you won't understand a word she says.

COLETTE (Sidonie-Gabrielle) (1873–1954)
French writer
In *Claudine and Annie*

When she raises her eyelids it's as if she were taking off all her clothes.

HANNAH COWLEY (1743–1809)
British poet and dramatist
In *Who's the Dupe?*

What is woman? – only one of Nature's agreeable blunders.

LADY CUNARD (Nancy) (1896–1965)
Writer and society hostess
On Margot Asquith

. . . black and wicked and with only a nodding acquaintance with the truth.

MARQUISE DU DEFFAND (1697–1780)
French noblewoman and wit
Quoted in Alfred Noyes' *Voltaire*,
On Marquise du Châtelet

She has worked so hard to appear what she is not, that she no longer knows what she really is.

EMILY DICKINSON (1830–1886)
American poet

Assent – and you are sane;
Demure – you're straightway dangerous
And handled with a Chain.

ISAK DINESEN (Karen Blixen) (1885–1962)
Danish novelist
In *Of Hidden Thoughts and of Heaven*

The entire being of a woman is a secret which should be kept.

GEORGE ELIOT (Marian Evans) (1819–1880)
British writer
In *Felix Holt*

Half the sorrows of women would be averted if they could repress the speech they know to be useless – nay, the speech they have resolved not to utter.

In *The Mill on the Floss*

The happiest women, like the happiest nations, have no history.

DAME EDITH EVANS (1888–1976)
British actress

When a woman behaves like a man, why doesn't she behave like a nice man?

On hearing that Nancy Mitford was borrowing a friend's villa in France 'to finish a book'.

Oh really? What's she reading?

ORIANA FALLACI (*b.* 1930)
Italian writer and journalist

I always introduce myself as . . . an encyclopedia of defects which I do not deny. Why should I? It took me a whole life to build myself as I am.

EDNA FERBER (1885–1968)
American writer and playwright

A woman can look both moral and exciting – if she also looks as if it was quite a struggle.

KATE FIELD (1838–1896)
Poet
In *Woman's Sphere*

They talk about a woman's sphere as though it had a limit;
There's not a place in earth or heaven,
There's not a task to mankind given,
There's not a blessing or a woe,
There's not a whispered 'yes' or 'no',

There's not a life, or death, or birth,
That has a feather's weight of worth
Without a woman in it.

FIFTH-GRADE GIRL
Quoted in *New York Times*, 12 June 1975

A woman can do anything a man can do – except be a grandfather, maybe.

HERMIONE GINGOLD (*b.* 1897)
British actress

Fighting is essentially a masculine idea; a woman's weapon is her tongue.

GERMAINE GREER (*b.* 1939)
Australian feminist
In *The Female Eunuch*

Man is jealous because of his *amour propre*; woman is jealous because of her lack of it.

Women are reputed never to be disgusted. The sad fact is that they often are, but not with men; they are most often disgusted with themselves.

MRS RONALD GREVILLE
Edwardian Society hostess
On Mrs Keppel, 1939

To hear Alice talk about her escape from France, one would have thought she had swum the Channel with her maid between her teeth.

LENA JEGER (*b.* 1915)
British politician

It's a sad woman that buys her own perfume.

ELIZABETH JENKINS (*b.* 1906)
British novelist and biographer

The woman whose behaviour indicates that she will make a scene if she is told the truth asks to be deceived.

JILL JOHNSTON (*b.* 1929)
American feminist

All women are lesbians, except those who don't know it yet.

ERICA JONG (*b.* 1942)
American writer
Quoted in *Time*, 1978

Women are the only exploited group in history who have been idealised into powerlessness.

SALLY KEMPTON (*b.* 1943)
American journalist

Women are the true maintenance class. Soceity is built upon their acquiescence and upon their small and necessary labours. The fact is that one cannot talk in feminist terms without revealing feelings which have been traditionally regarded as neurotic.

JEAN KERR (*b.* 1923)
American writer
In *The Snake Has all the Lines* ('How to Talk to a Man')

Women speak because they wish to speak, whereas a man speaks only when driven to speech by something outside himself – like, for instance, he can't find any clean socks.

ELSA LANCHESTER (*b.* 1902)
British actress
On Maureen O'Hara

She looked as though butter wouldn't melt in her mouth – or anywhere else.

FRAN LEBOWITZ (*b. circa* 1951)
American journalist
In *Metropolitan Life* ('Letters')

Being a woman is of special interest only to aspiring male transsexuals. To actual women, it is simply a good excuse not to play football.

ADA LEVERSON (1862–1933)
American writer

You don't know a woman until you have had a letter from her.

CLAUDIA LINNEAR
American singer

There are a lot of chicks who get laid by the director and still don't get the part.

ANITA LOOS (*b.* 1893)
American writer
In *Gentlemen Prefer Blondes*

Any girl who was a lady would not even think of having such a good time that she did not remember to hang on to her jewellery.

CLARE BOOTHE LUCE (*b.* 1903)
American writer and diplomat
On Greta Garbo:

A deer in the body of a woman, living resentfully in the Hollywood zoo.

Quoted in *New York Times*, 2 March 1969

Fortunately for woman, her body is still a trap – if no longer a baby trap, a man trap.

MARYA MANNES (*b.* 1904)
American novelist and poet
In *More in Anger* ('Introducing Myself')

The ultimate cynicism is to suspend judgement so that you are not judged.

MARY MCCARTHY (b. 1912)
American writer
In *On the Contrary* ('Characters in Fiction')

An interviewer asked me what book I thought best represented the modern American woman. All I could think of to answer was *Madame Bovary*.

I've never met a woman that I would regard as liberated who was at all strong for Women's Lib.

PHYLLIS MCGINLEY (*b.* 1905)
Canadian writer
On 'The Honour of Being a Woman'

Men may be allowed romanticism; women, who can create life in their own bodies, dare not indulge in it.

VIVIEN MERCHANT (1929–1982)
British actress
On her husband, Harold Pinter, leaving her for Lady Antonia Fraser

He didn't need to take a change of shoes. He can always wear hers. She has very big feet, you know.

NANCY MITFORD (1904–1973)
British writer
In *Love in a Cold Climate*

'Always be civil to the girls, you never know whom they may marry' is an aphorism which has saved many an English spinster from being treated like an Indian widow.

HANNAH MORE (1745–1833)
British writer and poet

Trifles made the sum of human things,
And half our misery from our foibles springs.

It is superfluous to decorate women highly for early youth; youth is itself a decoration. We mistakenly adorn most that part of life which least requires it, and neglect to provide for that which will want it most.

ROBIN MORGAN (*b.* 1941)
American feminist

Women are not inherently passive or peaceful. We're not inherently anything but human.

EDNA O'BRIEN (*b.* 1936)
Irish writer
Epigraph to Erica Jong's *Fear of Flying*

The vote, I thought, means nothing to women. We should be armed.

JACQUELINE KENNEDY ONASSIS (*b.* 1929)
Widow of US President, John F. Kennedy, and of Aristotle Onassis
Quoted by Eric F. Goldman, *The Tragedy of Lyndon Johnson*

Lady Bird would crawl down Pennsylvania Avenue on cracked glass for Lyndon Johnson.

DOROTHY PARKER (1893–1967)
American writer and wit
On Nan Britton, mistress of President Warren G. Harding

For when Miss Britton gets around to revealing, Lord, how she does reveal. She is one who kisses, among other things, and tells.

Most good women are hidden treasures who are only safe because nobody looks for them.

The affair between Margot Asquith and Margot Asquith will live as one of the prettiest love stories in all literature.

Katharine Hepburn ran the whole gamut of emotions from A to B.

Meeting Clare Boothe Luce in a doorway, Ms Boothe Luce made way, saying 'Age before beauty'. Said Ms Parker, gliding through the door, 'Pearls before swine!'

DIANE DE POITIERS (1499–1566)
Mistress of Henry II of France

The years that a woman subtracts from her age are not lost. They are added to other women's.

JACK POPPLEWELL
American writer
In *Every Other Evening*

Wife (borrowing mink coat from her husband's mistress): We shared the skunk – why not the mink?

GWEN RAVERAT (1885–1957)
British artist

I have defined ladies as people who did not do things themselves.

NANCY REAGAN (*b.* 1924)
Wife of US President Ronald Reagan

A woman is like a teabag – you can't tell how strong she is until you put her in hot water.

HELEN ROWLAND (1875–1950)
American journalist

The hardest task in a girl's life is to prove to a man that his intentions are serious.

ROSALIND RUSSELL (1908–1976)
American actress
Quoted in *New York Herald Tribune*, 11 April 1957

Flops are a part of life's menu and I've never been a girl to miss out on any of the courses.

MARY SCHARLIEB (1845–1930)
American writer
In *Reminiscences*
On pioneer women's doctor Elizabeth Garrett Anderson

Mrs Anderson . . . was a persistent, shameless and highly successful beggar.

HAZEL SCOTT
American feminist

Any woman who has a great deal to offer the world is in trouble.

CYBILL SHEPHERD
American actress
Quoted in *Daily Express*, 28 February 1978

Marilyn Monroe was all woman. She had curves in places other women don't even have places.

DAME EDITH SITWELL (1887–1964)
British poet
In a letter to Geoffrey Singleton, 11 July 1955

Virginia Woolf, I enjoyed talking to her, but thought *nothing* of her writing. I considered her 'a beautiful little knitter'.

CORNELIA OTIS SKINNER (1901–1979)
American actress

Woman's virtue is man's greatest invention.

GRACE SLICK (*b.* 1939)
American rock singer

The worst thing a little acid could do to Tricia Nixon is to turn her into a merely delightful person instead of a grinning robot.

NANCY BANKS SMITH
British journalist
In *The Guardian*, 8 January 1977

The most formidable headmaster I ever knew was a headmistress . . . She had X-ray pince-nez and that undivided bust popularized by Queen Mary. I think she was God in drag.

MRS GORDON SMITH
Quoted in Elizabeth Langhorne's *Nancy Astor and her Friends*

Nannie was a devout Christian Scientist, but not a good one. She kept confusing herself with God. She didn't know when to step aside and give God a chance.

PATTI SMITH (*b.* 1946)
American rock singer
The cross is just the true shape of a tortured woman.

FREYA STARK (*b.* 1893)
British traveller and writer
In *The Valleys of the Assassins*
The great and almost only comfort about being a woman is that one can always pretend to be more stupid than one is and no one is surprised.

MARY STOTT
British journalist
In *The Guardian*, 8 March 1983
I find it very heartening that of the women I have questioned lately about their feelings towards their mother, all the ones whose faces light up and who say 'She's wonderful' have been daughters of women who work outside the home.

IDA MINERVA TARBELL (1857–1944)
American journalist
Quoted in Mary E. Tomkins' *Ida M. Tarbell*
The only reason I am glad that I am a woman is that I will not have to marry one.

MARGARET THATCHER (*b.* 1925)
British politician
'Sayings of the Week' (*Observer*)
If your only opportunity is to be equal, then it is not equality.

MARGARET TURNBULL (*d.* 1942)
Scottish-born novelist
In *Alabaster Lamps*
No man is responsible for his father. That is entirely his mother's affair.

AMY VANDERBILT
Wealthy American Socialite

The modern rule is that every woman must be her own chaperone.

ROSALYN YALOW (*b.* 1921)
American doctor
Quoted in *Newsweek*, 29 October 1979

I think it's most unfortunate that we're learning about science from Jane Fonda.

THE INNER WOMAN – HEALTH AND NOURISHMENT

LADY (NANCY) ASTOR (1879–1964)
First woman to sit in the House of Commons

One reason I don't drink is that I want to know when I'm having a good time.

MARGARET ATWOOD (*b.* 1939)
Canadian novelist and poet

If the national mental illness of the United States is megalomania that of Canada is paranoid schizophrenia.

ARNOLD BENNETT (1867–1931)
British novelist
In *The Card*

'Ye can call it influenza if ye like,' said Mrs Machin. 'There was no influenza in my young days. We called a cold a cold.'

MADAME BENOIT

I feel a recipe is only a theme, which an intelligent cook can play each time with a variation.

ANGELINA BICOS

He eats like a horse afire.

BRITISH MEDICAL JOURNAL
Advertisement, 1960

'Distival can be given with complete safety to pregnant women and nursing mothers without adverse effect on mother or child.'

(Distival is also known as thalidomide.)

ERMA BOMBECK (*b.* 1927)
American writer

I am not a glutton – I am an explorer of food.

HELEN GURLEY BROWN (*b.* 1922)
American journalist

The only way you can stay as skinny as I am at my age is to starve.

JANE WELSH CARLYLE (1801–1866)
Wife of Thomas Carlyle
In a letter to John Welsh

Medical men all over the world having merely entered into a tacit agreement to call all sorts of maladies people are liable to, in cold weather, by one name; so that one sort of treatment may serve for all, and their practice be thereby greatly simplified.

RACHEL CARSON (1907–1964)
American scientific writer

The most alarming of all man's assaults upon the environment is the contamination of air, earth, rivers, and sea . . . this pollution is for the most part irrecoverable.

SHIRLEY CONRAN
British writer
In *Superwoman*, 1979

Life is too short to stuff a mushroom.

ADELLE DAVIS (1904–1974)
American health and cookery writer

If we now consider typical American meals with a critical eye, we see innocent stupidity elevated to an art.

Thousands upon thousands of persons have studied disease. Almost no one has studied health.

ELAINE DUNDY (*b.* 1937)
American writer
In *The Dud Avocado*

I hate champagne more than anything in the world next to Seven-Up.

EDNA FERBER (1885–1968)
American writer and playwright

'Roast beef medium' is not only a food. It's a philosophy.

BETTY FORD
Wife of former US President, Gerald Ford
'Sayings of the Week' (*Observer*) On alcohol

Maybe it picks you up a little bit, but it sure lets you down in a hurry.

US GIRL SCOUT MANUAL
'How Girls Can Help Their Country', 1913

Too soft a bed tends to make people dream which is unhealthy and weakening.

MRS HANNAH GLASSE (1708–1770)
British habitmaker and cookery writer

Take your hare when it is cased . . .

GAIL GREENE
American food critic and novelist

Great food is like great sex – the more you have the more you want.

J. P. GREENHILL
In *Office Gynaecology*

Woman is a constipated biped with a backache.

STORM JAMESON (Margaret) (*b.* 1891)
British novelist

She did not so much cook as assassinate food.

LARA JEFFERSON
Quoted in Otto Friedrich's *Going Crazy*

Here I sit – mad as the Hatter – with nothing to do but either become madder and madder or else recover enough of my sanity to be allowed to go back to the life which drove me mad.

GRACE JONES
Jamaican rock singer

I love oysters. It's my favourite food. I had a dozen oysters last night. I come to Paris just to eat oysters. Chile is another great place. I had three dozen of them over there.

JANIS JOPLIN (1943–1970)
American rock singer

I don't drink anything on the rocks. Cold is bad for my throat. So it's always straight or in tea. Southern Comfort tastes like orange petals in tea. I usually get about a pint and a half down me when I'm performing. Any more and I start to nod.

JEAN KERR (*b.* 1923)
American writer

If you have formed the habit of checking on every new diet that comes along, you will find that, mercifully, they all blur together, leaving you with only one definite piece of information: french fried potatoes are out.

EARTHA KITT (*b.* 1928)
American singer

People these days are thinking less and drinking more.

JINNIE LANE

The doc says I have a slight case of conspicuous consumption.

FRAN LEBOWITZ (*b. circa* 1951)
American journalist

Food is an important part of a balanced diet.

Vegetables are interesting but lack a sense of purpose when unaccompanied by a good cut of meat.

ROSE MACAULAY (1889–1958)
British writer

Gentlemen know that fresh air should be kept in its proper place – out of doors – and that, God having given us indoors and out-of-doors, we should not attempt to do away with this distinction.

HARRIET MARTINEAU (1802–1876)
British writer

Men who pass most comfortably through the world are those who possess good digestions and hard hearts.

DR JEAN MAYER (*b.* 1920)
French scientist

Attributing overweight to over-eating is hardly more illuminating than ascribing alcoholism to alcohol.

MIGNON MCLAUGHLIN
American writer

I'm glad I don't have to explain to a man from Mars why each day I set fire to dozens of little pieces of paper, and then put them in my mouth.

MARILYN MONROE (1926–1962)
American actress
Quoted by Sir Laurence Olivier
On having matzo balls for dinner for the third time at Arthur Miller's parents

Isn't there any other part of a matzo you can eat?

MISS PIGGY'S GUIDE TO LIFE (as told to Henry Beard)
Television puppet

When one is as busy with a career as moi, one has to rely on professionals to handle the more time-consuming aspects of one's exercise program. I have a very nice man who operates this lovely machinery for me and there is a perfectly charming young lady who comes in twice a week to do yoga for me. They are such a help.

COUNTESS MORPHY
English aristocrat

Plain cooking cannot be entrusted to plain cooks.

FRIEDRICH WILHELM NIETZSCHE (1844–1900)
German philosopher

The sick woman especially; no one surpasses her in refinements for ruling, oppressing, tyrannising.

NELLIE NORTON

They served the most abdominal cocktails.

DOROTHY PARKER (1893–1967)
American writer and wit
Quoted in her obituary in *New York Times*, 8 June 1967

As far as I'm concerned, the most beautiful word in the English language is cellar-door.

HESTER LYNCH PIOZZI (Mrs Thrale) (1741–1821)
In a letter to Fanny Burney, 12 November 1781

A physician can sometimes parry the scythe of death, but has no power over the sand in the hourglass.

GILDA RADNER

Eating is self-punishment; punish the food instead. Strangle a loaf of Italian bread. Throw darts at a cheesecake. Chain a lamb chop to the bed. Beat up a cookie.

LINDA RONSTADT (*b.* 1946)
American rock singer

Running is the best, and I think the only, cure for depression. There have never been any drugs I could take that would make depression go away.

HELEN ROWLAND (1875–1950)
American journalist

Ever since Eve started it all by offering Adam the apple, woman's punishment has been to have to supply a man with food and then suffer the consequences when it disagrees with him.

In *A Guide to Men*

There is a vast difference between the savage and the civilized man, but it is never apparent to their wives until after breakfast.

HELENA RUBENSTEIN (1871–1965)
French cosmetician

Diet is a way of eating for the kind of life you want.

GLORIA RUSSAKOV

All it takes to be a restaurant critic in Portland is being able to tell which frozen cheesecake is Sara Lee.

MRS CHARLES H. SABIN

The prohibition law, written for weaklings and derelicts, has divided the nation, like Gaul, into three parts – wets, drys and hypocrites.

SAKI (Hector Hugh Munro) (1870–1916)
British novelist

The cook was a good cook, as cooks go; and as cooks go she went.

BEVERLY SILLS (*b.* 1929)
American singer and opera director

There are an awful lot of skinny people in the cemetery.

DODIE SMITH (*b.* 1896)
British writer

Noble deeds and hot baths are the best cures for depression.

SUSAN SONTAG (*b.* 1933)
American writer

Illness is the night-side of life, a more onerous citizenship. Everyone who is born holds dual citizenship, in the kingdom of the well and in the kingdom of the sick. Although we all prefer to use only the good passport, sooner or later each of us is obliged, at least for a spell, to indentify ourselves as citizens of that other place.

SPANISH PROVERB

An ailing woman lives for ever.

BARBARA STRAUS (–1975)

It's time to button down the hatches, or is it batten down the hedges?

JACQUELINE SUSANN (1921–1974)
American novelist

Cigarettes give you cancer, heart trouble and everything else. But pot has a built-in safety device; three cigarettes and you gotta pass out.

ELIZABETH TAYLOR (1912–1975)
British writer
In *At Mrs Lippincote's*

How did this notion get round that women cook only for men? Why, indeed, should we manage with some cheese just because our sexual organs are different?

ALICE B. TOKLAS (1877–1967)
American cookery writer

What is sauce for the goose may be sauce for the gander but it is not necessarily sauce for the chicken, the duck, the turkey, or the guinea hen.

LILY TOMLIN (*b.* 1939)
American comedienne

For fast-acting relief try slowing down.

JESSICA TUCHMAN
Quoted in *Newsweek*, 20 June 1977

In much of the world the chief human right that people recognize is 800 calories a day.

ABIGAIL VAN BUREN (*b.* 1918)
American agony columnist

Psychotherapy, unlike castor oil which will work no matter how you get it down, is useless when forced on an uncooperative patient.

HARRIET VAN HORNE
American columnist
Quoted in *Vogue*, 1956

Cooking is like love – it should be entered into with abandon, or not at all.

MRS JOSEPHINE CURTIS WOODBURY
In *Arena*, 1899
On Mary Baker Eddy, founder of the Church of Christ Scientist

What she has really 'discovered' are ways and means of perverting and prostituting the science of healing to her own ecclesiastical aggrandizement, and to the moral and physical depravity of her dupes.

VIRGINIA WOOLF (1882–1941)
British writer

And now with some pleasure I find that it's seven; and must cook dinner. Haddock and sausage meat. I think it is true that one gains a certain hold on sausage and haddock by writing them down.

In *A Room of One's Own*

One cannot think well, love well, sleep well, if one has not dined well.

EDITH ZITTLER

The only way to stop smoking is to just stop – no ifs, ands or butts.

THE OUTER WOMAN – BEAUTY AND FASHION

ALISON ADBURGHAM
On Queen Victoria

It was not that she herself was a fashion leader. Probably the most notable garment she ever wore was the nightdress in which she received, that early morning at Kensington Palace, the news of her uncle's death – the nightdress in which she became Queen.

ELIZABETH ARDEN (*circa* 1884–1966)
Canadian cosmetician

Nothing that costs only a dollar is worth having.

JOAN ARMATRADING (*b.* 1950)
British singer

I know I'm black. I see it all the time, I like it, I wouldn't want to wash it off. I mean, some of my family are black.

LUCIANA AVEDON

There will always be glamorous women who declare that they do nothing special to maintain their trim, attractive bodies; a zest for living is what keeps you young, they proclaim. I do not envy them; I just don't believe a word they say.

CRISTOBAL BALENCIAGA (*b.* 1892)
Spanish couturière
Quoted in *Sunday Telegraph*, 1968

If you want publicity – add a touch of vulgarity.

WAY BANDY

What does a woman need to know in order to design her face with cosmetics? Only her skin and her bones.

CECIL BEATON (1904–1980)
British photographer and designer
On the mini skirt

Never in the history of fashion has so little material been raised so high to reveal so much that needs to be covered so badly.

ALAN BENNETT (*b.* 1934)
British playwright

One of the few lessons I have learned in life is that there is invariably something odd about women who wear ankle socks.

AMBROSE BIERCE (1842–1916?)
American writer and journalist
In *The Devil's Dictionary*

Beauty, *n.* The power by which a woman charms a lover and terrifies a husband.

LOUISE BROOKS (*b.* 1900)
American actress

Most beautiful but dumb girls think they are smart and get away with it, because other people, on the whole, aren't much smarter.

HELEN GURLEY BROWN (*b.* 1922)
American journalist

Some of us are not great beauties. That notion is entirely responsible for whatever success I have had in life, because not being beautiful, I had to make up for it with brains, charm, drive, personality – you name it.

R. W. BUCHANAN (1841–1901)
British poet

She just wore
Enough for modesty – no more.

RICHARD BURTON (*b.* 1925)
British actor
On Elizabeth Taylor

She is an extremely beautiful woman, lavishly endowed by nature with but a few flaws in the masterpiece; she has an incipient double-chin, her legs are too short, and she has a slight pot-belly. She has a wonderful bosom though.

LORD BYRON (1788–1824)
British poet
On novelist Maria Edgeworth

She was a nice little unassuming 'Jeanie Deans-looking body' as we Scotch say – and, if not handsome, certainly not ill-looking. Her conversation was as quiet as herself. One would never have guessed she could write *her name*.

COCO CHANEL (Gabrielle) (1883–1971)
French couturière

Wearing her skirt halfway up the thigh does not give a woman the advantage.

Saint Laurent has excellent taste. The more he copies me, the better taste he displays.

Fashion is made to become unfashionable.

When I started, at least women dressed to please men. Now they dress to astonish one another.

If fashion isn't worn by everybody, then it is only eccentricity.

EDNA WOOLMAN CHASE
American fashion journalist

Fashion can be bought. Style one must possess.

MALCOLM DE CHAZAL

Women always show more taste in their choice of underclothing than in their choice of jewellery.

LORD CHESTERFIELD (1694–1773)
British statesman and letter-writer
In *Letters to His Son*, 5 September 1748

Women who are either indisputably beautiful, or indisputably ugly, are best flattered upon the score of their understanding.

G. K. CHESTERTON (1874–1936)
British essayist and novelist
On the sculptor Phidias (*circa* 490–430 BC)

There was an old sculptor named Phidias
Whose knowledge of art was invidious
He carved Aphrodite
Without any nightie—
Which startled the purely fastidious.

JENNIE JEROME CHURCHILL (1854–1921)
In Anita Leslie's *Jennie*
On herself, in conversation with her sister Leonie

I shall never get used to not being the most beautiful woman in the room. It was an intoxication to sweep in and know every man had turned his head. It kept me in form.

ANITA COLBY
Quoted in *Cosmopolitan*, 1968

Before you go out, always take off something you've put on, because you probably are wearing too much.

HARTLEY COLERIDGE (1796–1849)
British writer and son of Samuel T. Coleridge

She is not fair to outward view
As many maidens be;
Her loveliness I never knew
Until she smiled on me.

LADY DIANA COOPER (*b.* 1892)
English aristocrat
Quoted in *International Herald Tribune*

I was known as a great beauty because I had a knack for

attracting publicity. I was always falling through a skylight or holding a camel, wearing evening dress.

LILY DACHE (*b.* 1904)
American couturière

Glamour is what makes a man ask for your telephone number. But it also is what makes a woman ask for the name of your dressmaker.

ANGIE DICKINSON (*b.* 1931)
American actress

I dress for women – and I undress for men.

EMILY DICKINSON (1830–1886)
American poet

Beauty – be not caused – It is,
Chase it, and it ceases;
Chase it not, and it abides.

MARLENE DIETRICH (*b.* 1901)
German actress

The relationship between the make-up man and the film actor is one of accomplices in crime.

The average man is more interested in a woman who is interested in him than he is in a woman – any woman – with beautiful legs.

PHYLLIS DILLER (*b.* 1917)
American comedienne

It's an ill wind that blows when you leave the hairdresser.
It's a good thing that beauty is only skin deep, or I'd be rotten to the core.

CHRISTIAN DIOR (1905–1957)
French couturier

There is no such thing as an ugly woman – there are only the ones who do not know how to make themselves attractive.

BRITT EKLAND
Swedish actress

I like Bianca Jagger because she is one of the few women I know who has as much class and style as I have.

I'm so happy – it's so nice to go with a man whose clothes you can wear.

GEORGE ELIOT (Marian Evans) (1819–1880)
British novelist
In *Amos Barton*

Boots and shoes are the greatest trouble of my life. Everything else one can turn and turn about, and make old look like new; but there's no coaxing boots and shoes to look better than they are.

RALPH WALDO EMERSON (1803–1881)
American writer

I have heard with admiring submission the experience of the lady who declared that the sense of being well-dressed gives a feeling of inward tranquillity which religion is powerless to bestow.

A beautiful woman is a practical poet.

ERTE (Romain de Tirtoff) (*b.* 1892)
French designer
Quoted in the *Guardian*, 1975

A resourceful woman who is almost downright plain can achieve the reputation of a beauty simply by announcing to everybody she meets that she is one.

The feminine body is essentially a malleable entity which fashion moulds in its own way.

GEORGE FARQUHAR (1677–1707)
Irish dramatist
In *The Beaux' Stratagem*

No woman can be a beauty without a fortune.

F. SCOTT FITZGERALD (1896–1940)
American writer
In a letter to his daughter, Frances Scott Fitzgerald

A great social success is a pretty girl who plays her cards as carefully as if she were plain.

ANATOLE FRANCE (1844–1924)
French writer
In *The Crime of Sylvestre Bonnard*

Ugly women may be naturally quite as capricious as pretty ones, but as they are never petted and spoiled, and as no allowances are made for them, they soon find themselves obliged either to suppress their whims or to hide them.

HERMIONE GINGOLD (*b.* 1897)
British actress

Contrary to popular belief, English women do not wear tweed nightgowns.

MADAME DE GIRARDIN (1806–1881)
Wife of the French politician and journalist Emile de Girardin

There is only one proper way to wear a beautiful dress: to forget you are wearing it.

JEAN GIRAUDOUX (1882–1944)
French writer
In *Ondine*

A pretty woman has the right to be ignorant of everything, provided she knows when to keep still.

EMMA GOLDMAN (1869–1940)
American anarchist

I'd rather have roses on my table than diamonds on my neck.

PRUDENCE GLYNN (*b.* 1935)
British journalist
In *The Times*, 1980

Style is something other people have. The merest inkling that you yourself may be in possession of the commodity is enough to ensure that you are not, for style, like the Victoria Cross, is an accolade which must be bestowed by the recognition of a third party.

OLIVER GOLDSMITH (1728–1774)
British poet and playwright
In *She Stoops to Conquer*

A modest woman, dressed out in all her finery, is the most tremendous object of the whole creation.

BETTY GRABLE (1916–1973)
American actress

There are two reasons why I'm in show business, and I'm standing on both of them.

GRACIAN (1601–1658)
Spanish writer and philosopher

A beautiful woman should break her mirror early.

JOYCE GRENFELL (1910–1980)
British actress and comedienne

Clothes? Oh yes, I like clothes – on other people. Well, somehow they seem to suffer a sea-change when they get on to me. They look quite promising in the shop; and not entirely without hope when I get them back into my wardrobe. But then, when I put them on they tend to deteriorate with a very strange rapidity and one feels sorry for them.

FIORELLO LA GUARDIA
Former Mayor of New York
'Sayings of the Week' (*Observer*, 19 July 1942)

British women are rosy-cheeked and healthy, but somehow they can't seem to keep their stockings right.

MARGARET HALSEY (*b.* 1910)
American writer

Englishwomen's shoes look as if they had been made by someone who had often heard shoes described, but had never seen any.

DEBBIE HARRY (*b.* 1941)
American rock singer

I was sort of weird. I had my hair bleached white all over with a vegetable colouring and I used to wear black every day. I was an art student.

On her legs

Ugh! I pluck them, one hair at a time. I like the pain.

H. HASKINS
American writer

If a man hears much that a woman says, she is not beautiful.

KATHARINE HEPBURN (*b.* 1909)
American actress

Plain women know more about men than beautiful ones do.

ROBERT HERRICK (1591–1674)
British cleric and poet
In 'Delight in Disorder'

A sweet disorder in the dress . . .

EDGAR WATSON HOWE (1853–1937)
In *Country Town Sayings*

A man has his clothes made to fit him; a woman makes herself fit her clothes.

FRANK MCKINNEY HUBBARD (1868–1930)
American writer

A woman will buy anything she thinks a store is losing money on.

VIRGINIA CARY HUDSON
American writer
In *O Ye Jigs and Juleps*

Personal appearance is looking the best you can for the money.

H. HUGHES
Writer
In *Fragments on Women*

No woman can be handsome by the force of features alone, any more than she can be witty only by the help of speech.

MARGARET HUNGERFORD (1855–1897)
Quoted in *Molly Bawn*

Beauty is in the eye of the beholder.

ITALIAN PROVERB

She who is born a beauty is born betrothed.

BIANCA JAGGER
Former wife of pop singer Mick Jagger

I don't think chic has anything to do with money. You can have all the money in the world and have no idea what elegance means.

JACQUELINE KENNEDY ONASSIS (*b.* 1929)
Widow of US President John F. Kennedy and of Aristotle Onassis
On being accused of spending $30,000 a year on her wardrobe *circa* 1963

I couldn't spend that much unless I wore sable underwear.

JOHN F. KENNEDY (1917–1963)
35th President of the United States of America
On receiving a $40,000 bill for his wife's clothes

Is there such a thing as Shoppers Anonymous?

JEAN KERR (*b.* 1923)
American writer
In *The Snake Has all the Lines*

I'm tired of all this nonsense about beauty being only skin-deep. That's deep enough. What do you want – an adorable pancreas?

LADIES HOME JOURNAL, 1947

The average girl would rather have beauty than brains because she knows that the average man can see much better than he can think.

HEDY LAMARR (*b.* 1913)
Austrian film star

Any girl can be glamorous; all you have to do is stand still and look stupid.

JAMES LAVER (1899–1975)
British novelist
Quoted in *Newsweek*, 16 March 1970

The same costume will be indecent 10 years before its time, smart in its time, dowdy one year after its time, ridiculous 20 years after its time, quaint 50 years after its time, romantic 100 years after its time and beautiful 150 years after its time.

GIOVANNI LEONE (*b.* 1908)
Italian academic and politician

The strongest evidence to prove that God exists is a beautiful woman.

MARY WILSON LITTLE
American writer

It is difficult to see why lace should be so expensive; it is mostly holes.

EDITH RAYMOND LOCK
Fashion editor
Quoted in *Stores*, May 1970

Fashion is the business that turns mystique into blue-chip stocks, obsolescence into dollars, and a hemline revolution into profit.

CAROLE LOMBARD (1908–1942)
Quoted in Malcolm Muggeridge's *The Sun Never Sets*

I live by a man's code, designed to fit a man's world, yet at the same time I never forget that a woman's first job is to choose the right shade of lipstick.

SOPHIA LOREN (*b.* 1934)
Italian actress

Women who live for the next miracle cream do not realize that beauty comes from a secret happiness and equilibrium within themselves.

Today a man can see practically the whole woman at a single glance. It's swallowing a meal at one mouthful.

EDNA ST VINCENT MILLAY (1892–1950)
American poet

A man's habit clings
And he will wear tomorrow what today he wears.

JEAN BAPTISTE MOLIÈRE (1622–1673)
French playwright
In *The School for Wives*

Wives rarely fuss about their beauty
To guarantee their mate's affection.

MARY TYLER MOORE (*b.* 1936)
American actress

Behind each beautiful wild fur there is an ugly story. It is a brutal, bloody and barbaric story. The animal is not killed – it is tortured. I don't think a fur coat is worth it.

JULIA MORLEY
British organizer of 'Miss World'

If it is a flesh market, you won't find finer flesh anywhere.

MALCOLM MUGGERIDGE (*b.* 1903)
British journalist
In *The Most of Malcolm Muggeridge* ('Women of America')

American women: How they mortify the flesh in order to make it appetizing! Their beauty is a vast industry, their enduring allure a discipline which nuns or athletes might find excessive.

OLIVIA NEWTON-JOHN (*b.* 1948)
English-born *American singer*

I'm a trouser person, really.

SUSIE ORBACH (*b.* 1946)
American writer

Fat is a Feminist Issue (book title)

OVID (43 BC–AD 18)
Latin poet
In *The Art of Beauty*

Dear to the heart of a girl is her own beauty and charm.

DOROTHY PARKER (1893–1967)
American writer and wit
In *Enough Rope*

Where's the man could ease a heart
Like a satin gown?

Horsie: All I say is, nobody has any business to go around looking like a horse and behaving as if it were all right. You don't catch horses going around looking like people, do you?

SUZY PARKER (*b.* 1933)
Quoted in *Newsweek*, February 1963

I got a coat lined with hamster. You couldn't do that kind of thing in America. All the Boy Scouts would go on strike.

DOLLY PARTON (*b.* 1946)
American country singer

I like looking as if I came out of a fairy tale.

I wasn't born with a wig and make-up and I could be very stylish if I chose to be. But I would never stoop so low as to be *fashionable*.

ELSA PERETTI

Energy is beauty – a Ferrari with an empty tank doesn't run.

MISS PIGGY'S GUIDE TO LIFE (as told to Henry Beard)
Television puppet
Make-up Rules I Made Up – Don't Break Them!

With so many different kinds of cosmetics and so many different types of colouring, shading, and toning that can be achieved by using them, there simply is no one correct make-up method. What's right for moi may not be right for you (for example, you probably use a little less ear-liner). However, what is *wrong* for moi is definitely wrong for you too. Consult my Ten Tone Commandments. If you avoid these make-up sins, chances are your appearance will be heavenly.

I. Never use yellow lipstick.
II. Never put anything on your face that comes in a can.
III. Never purchase beauty products in hardware stores.
IV. Never colour your teeth.
V. Never put flowers in your nose.
VI. Never put anything blue on your cheeks.
VII. Never use anything that stinks, stings, or stains.

VIII. Never use anything that makes you cry, sneeze, look old, or turn red and bumpy.
IX. Never braid your eyelashes.
X. Never powder your tongue.

PLAUTUS (250–184 BC)
Roman playwright

A woman smells well when she smells of nothing.

PROPERTIUS (*circa* 48–*circa* 15 BC)
Roman poet

If she is pleasing to one man, a girl is taken care of.

MARY QUANT (*b.* 1934)
British fashion designer
On the fashionable woman

She is sexy, witty, and dry-cleaned.

GILDA RADNER

I base most of my fashion taste on what doesn't itch.

REX REED (*b.* 1938)
American journalist
On Sophia Loren

What a subject: her nose is too big, her mouth is too big, she has the composites of all the wrong things, but put them all together and pow! All the natural mistakes of beauty fall together to create a magnificent accident.

LENI RIEFENSTAHL
German film-maker

We all want to be beautiful.

ROBERT RILEY
Quoted in *New York Times*, 12 December 1973

In the 1920s it was legs. My God, women hadn't shown their legs for 2,000 years.

MAX ROBERTSON
Contemporary radio commentator
Attributed during a BBC commentary on Wimbledon Lawn Tennis Tournament

Here comes Queen Ingrid looking beautiful in an off-the-hat face.

HELEN ROWLAND (1875–1950)
American journalist

The softer a man's head, the louder his socks.

HELENA RUBENSTEIN (1871–1965)
French cosmetician

There are no ugly women, only lazy ones.

FRANÇOISE SAGAN (*b.* 1936)
French novelist
Quoted in *The Observer*, 14 December 1969

A dress has no meaning unless it makes a man want to take it off.

YVES SAINT LAURENT (*b.* 1936)
French couturier

The most beautiful make-up of a woman is passion. But cosmetics are easier to buy.

My clothes are addressed to women who can afford to travel with forty suitcases.

What is important in a dress is the woman who's wearing it.

CARL SANDBURG (1878–1967)
American poet
In *Cool Tombs*

Pocahontas' body, lovely as a poplar, sweet as a red haw in November or a pawpaw in May.

ELSA SCHIAPARELLI (1890–1975)
Italian-born couturière
Quoted in *Newsweek*, 29 March 1971

In difficult times fashion is always outrageous.

WILLIAM SHAKESPEARE (1564–1616)
English playwright

A woman moved is like a fountain troubled
Muddy, ill-seeming, thick, bereft of beauty.

GEORGE BERNARD SHAW (1856–1950)
Irish playwright

Remember always that the least plain sister is the family beauty.

EUGENIA SHEPPARD
American journalist
Quoted in *New York Herald Tribune*, 13 January 1960

To call a fashion wearable is the kiss of death. No new fashion worth its salt is ever wearable.

DAME EDITH SITWELL (1887–1964)
British poet

The trouble with most Englishwomen is that they *will* dress as if they had been a mouse in a previous incarnation . . . they do not want to attract attention.

Quoted in *New York Times*, 1962

Good taste is the worse vice ever invented.

In *Taken Care Of*, 1956

Vulgarity is, in reality, nothing but a modern chic, part descendant of the goddess Dullness.

On *Why I Look as I Do*

Why not be oneself? That is the whole secret of a successful appearance. If one is a greyhound, why try to look like a Pekingese?

MARTHA SLITER
American journalist
Quoted in *Advertising Age*, 13 April 1959

A hat is the difference between wearing clothes and wearing a costume; it's the difference between being dressed – and being dressed up; it's the difference between looking adequate and looking your best.

HELEN VAN SLYKE
American novelist
Quoted in *New York Times*, 28 August 1963

The rush of power to the head is not as becoming as a new hat.

STEVIE SMITH (1902–1971)
British poet
In *This Englishwoman*

This Englishwoman is so refined
She has no bosom and no behind.

CARMEL SNOW (1980–1961)
American fashion journalist
In *The World of Carmel Snow*

Elegance is good taste, *plus* a dash of daring.

RICHARD STEELE (1672–1729)
British essayist
In *The Spectator*, 1711–12

No woman is capable of being beautiful who is not incapable of being false.

TOM STOPPARD (*b.* 1937)
British playwright
In *Travesties*

Unrelieved truthfulness can give a young girl a reputation for insincerity. I have known plain girls with nothing to hide, captivate the London season purely by discriminate mendacity.

DOWAGER LADY SWAYTHLING (*b.* 1908)
'Sayings of the Week' (*Observer*, 23 May 1937)

It was said that in the Victorian days it took two sheep to clothe one woman: today all her clothing is provided from one silkworm.

JONATHAN SWIFT (1667–1745)
British satirist

She wears her clothes as if they were thrown on her with a pitchfork.

ALFRED LORD TENNYSON (1809–1892)
British poet
In *A Dream of Fair Women*

A daughter of the gods, divinely tall,
And most divinely fair.

JOHN TOBIN (1770–1804)
British playwright
In *The Honeymoon*

She's adorned
Amply that in her husband's eye looks lovely.

LILY TOMLIN (*b.* 1939)
American comedienne

If truth is beauty, how come no one has their hair done in the library?

MARK TWAIN (Samuel Langhorne Clemens) (1835–1910)
American writer
In *Autobiography*

A thoroughly beautiful woman and a thoroughly homely woman are creations which I love to gaze upon, and which I cannot tire of gazing upon, for each is perfect in her own line.

THORSTEIN VEBLEN (1857–1929)
Writer
In *The Theory of the Leisure Class*

The corset is, in economic theory, substantially a mutilation, undergone for the purpose of lowering the subject's vitality and rendering her permanently and obviously unfit for work.

The womanliness of woman's apparel resolves itself into the more effective hindrance to useful exertion offered by the garments peculiar to women.

JILL TWEEDIE
British journalist

You don't have to signal a social conscience by looking like a frump. Lace knickers won't hasten the holocaust . . . There is not much fun in the world today which is all the more reason to cherish what little there is and fashion is fun.

DIANA VREELAND (*b. circa* 1901)
American fashion journalist
Quoted in *Esquire*, 1965

You know, don't you, that the bikini is only the most important thing since the atom bomb.

I've never thought of fashion as being anything but young, because when it is old, it's a compromise. Then it's no longer fashion, it's merchandise.

Quoted in *Newsweek*, 10 December 1962

The only real elegance is in the mind; if you've got that, the rest really comes from it.

Quoted in *Rolling Stone*, 11 August 1977

Pink is the navy blue of India.

I don't think the American woman has any vestige of originality or any special thing of her own. Nor does she want them. Let's face it, all she wants is to be popular.

EDMUND WALLER (1606–1687)
British poet
In *On a Lady Passing through a Crowd of People*

The yielding marble of her snowy breast.

MARY WARNOCK (*b.* 1923)
Research Fellow, Oxford University

The implication (in women's magazines) is that once you are over forty it doesn't matter what you wear. There is rarely an article written about women over fifty that does not envisage a steady, and if possible graceful, decline into old age, all passion spent, and with the frivolities of sex, scent, clothes all now subjects only of observation in others, not of living experience.

SIMONE WEIL (1909–1943)
French philosopher
On 'Gravity and Grace'

Beauty is a fruit which we look at without trying to seize it.

JUNE WEIR
Quoted in *New York Times*, 15 August 1976

Why do women pay attention to fashion? Because we all wear clothes, that's why.

TUESDAY WELD (*b.* 1943)
American actress

Fashion is finding something you're comfortable in and wearing it into the ground.

KATHARINE WHITEHORN
British journalist
In *Shouts and Murmurs*, a selection from the *Observer*

Hats divide generally into three classes: offensive hats, defensive hats, and shrapnel.

OSCAR WILDE (1854–1900)
Irish writer
In *Lady Windermere's Fan*

A man who moralises is usually a hypocrite, and a woman who moralises is invariably plain.

TOYAH WILLCOX (*b.* 1958)
British actress and rock singer

George Cukor asked me 'Please take off your hat' and I said 'That's my hair!' Then he said, 'Excuse me' and went next door. From behind the door I could hear roars of laughter – but I got the part in the end.

WILLIAM CARLOS WILLIAMS (1883–1963)
American poet and novelist
In *Pictures from Brueghel*

All women are not Helen . . . but have Helen in their hearts.

DUCHESS OF WINDSOR (*b.* 1896)
Also attributed to Mrs William Paley and Truman Capote

No woman can be too rich or too thin.

SHELLEY WINTERS (*b.* 1922)
American actress
Quoted in *The Sunday Times*, 1971

Plunging necklines attract more attention and cost less money.

MEN

SHANA ALEXANDER
Contemporary American journalist and broadcaster
I don't believe man is woman's natural enemy. Perhaps his lawyer is.

LISA ALTHER (*b.* 1944)
American writer
In *Kinflicks*
She had learnt . . . that it was impossible to discuss issues civilly with a person who insisted on referring to himself as 'we'.

MARGOT ASQUITH (1865–1945)
British society hostess
On David Lloyd George
He couldn't see a belt without hitting below it.

On F. E. Smith
Very clever, but his brains go to his head.

SIMONE DE BEAUVOIR (*b.* 1908)
French writer
Quoted in the *Observer*, 1974
If any man had proved sufficiently self-centred and commonplace to attempt my subjugation, I should have judged him, found him wanting and left him. The only sort of person in whose favour I could ever wish to surrender my autonomy would be just the one who did his utmost to prevent any such thing.

DUCHESS OF BEDFORD
'Sayings of the Week' (*Observer*, 8 December 1974)
Men must be the leaders. That's why they have glorious

plumage, like peacocks, and the little grey females must go where they direct.

MOLLY BERKELEY
In *Beaded Bubbles*

But from then on he (the Earl of Berkeley) began giving me things. A house in California, a beautiful villa in Rome and other such gadgets.

HELEN BEVINGTON
In *Along Came the Witch*

I don't feel like a survivor, I feel left behind.

HONOR BLACKMAN (*b.* 1926)
British actress

Men who are insecure about their masculinity often challenge me to fights.

MARGARET BOSWELL (–1789)
Wife of James Boswell
On her husband's attachment to Dr Johnson, 1773

I have often seen a bear led by a man, but never till now have I seen a man led by a bear.

KATHERINE BRADLEY (1848–1914) and
EDITH COOPER (1862–1913)
In *Journals*
On George Moore

His smile is like sunshine on putty.

COMTESSE DE BRÉMONT
French society hostess
To W. S. Gilbert, on hearing that before agreeing to an interview he would require a fee of twenty guineas

The Comtesse de Brémont presents her compliments to Mr W. S. Gilbert and in reply to his answer to her request for an interview for *St Paul's* in which he states his terms as twenty guineas for that privilege, begs to say that she anticipates the pleasure of writing his obituary for nothing.

BRIGID BROPHY (*b.* 1929)
Irish writer

I refuse to consign the whole male sex to the nursery. I insist on believing that some men are my equals.

ELIZABETH BARRETT BROWNING (1806–1861)
British poet
In *Aurora Leigh*

Men get opinions as boys learn to spell
By reiteration chiefly.

SUSAN BROWNMILLER (*b.* 1935)
American feminist
In *Against Our Will*

Rape is . . . nothing more or less than a conscious process of intimidation by which all men keep all women in a state of fear.

CYNTHIA BUCHANAN
Quoted in *New York Times*, 9 February 1972

What have Hemingway and Hefner and Bogart and (even) John Kennedy and Charles Atlas and the sins of our fathers before them done to our males that they continue to labour under their own ghostly machismo? – which must be the loneliest, most fragile state in the world, this worship of form without content.

EDITH BUNKER
Fictional character in American TV series

Archie doesn't know how to worry without getting upset.

FANNY BURNEY (Madame D'Arblay) (1752–1840)
English novelist and diarist
In her *Diary*, 23 August 1778

Indeed, the freedom with which Dr Johnson condemns whatever he disapproves is astonishing.

HORTENSE CALISHER (*b.* 1911)
American novelist

When a man begins to *act* logically according to others . . . then he has left his youth behind.

MRS PATRICK CAMPBELL (1865–1940)
British actress
In a letter to George Bernard Shaw, 1 November 1912

Oh dear me – it's too late to do anything but *accept* you and *love* you – but when you were quite a little boy somebody ought to have said 'hush' just once.

In a letter to George Bernard Shaw, January 1913
On J. M. Barrie

A little child whom the Gods have whispered to.

JANE WELSH CARLYLE (1801–1866)
Wife of Thomas Carlyle
In a letter to her husband

If they had said the sun or the moon had gone out of the heavens, it could not have struck me with the idea of a more awful and dreary blank in the creation than the words: Byron is dead.

LADY VIOLET BONHAM CARTER (1887–1969)
British politician
On Stafford Cripps

Sir Stafford has a brilliant mind – until it is made up.

ALICE CARY (1820–1871)
In *Make Believe*

Kiss me, though you make believe;
  Kiss me, though I almost know
You are kissing to deceive.

ILKA CHASE (*b.* 1905)
American actress and writer

When he said we were trying to make a fool of him, I could only murmur that the Creator had beat us to it.

ANNE BIGOT DE CORNUEL (1605–1694)
French writer

No man is a hero to his valet.

NOËL COWARD (1899–1973)
British actor and playwright
On meeting Edna Ferber, who was wearing a suit similar to his own

Edna, you look almost like a man.
'So do you,' answered Miss Ferber.

KATHRYN CRAVENS
In *Pursuit of Gentlemen*

If a man is vain, flatter. If timid, flatter. If boastful, flatter. In all history, too much flattery never lost a gentleman.

CONSTANCE CUMMINGS (*b.* 1910)
American actress
Quoted in Michael Foot's *Aneurin Bevan*
On Aneurin Bevan

He was like a fire in a room on a cold winter's day.

MARY KYLE DALLAS (1837–1897)
In *After Ten Years*

Man never quite forgets his very first love,
    Unless she's true.

NIGEL DENNIS (*b.* 1912)
British writer
In *Cards of Identity*

This man, she reasons, as she looks at her husband, is a poor fish. But he is the nearest I can get to the big one that got away.

MARLENE DIETRICH (*b.* 1901)
German actress

Once a woman has forgiven her man, she must not reheat his sins for breakfast.

MARY ABIGAIL DODGE (1836–1896)
American feminist
In *Both Sides*

What's virtue in man can't be vice in a cat.

MAMIE VAN DOREN (*b.* 1933)
American actress
In *Quote and Unquote*

It is possible that blondes also prefer gentlemen.

GEORGE ELIOT (Marian Evans) (1819–1880)
British novelist
In *Janet's Repentance*

Any coward can fight a battle when he's sure of winning; but give me the man who has pluck to fight when he's sure of losing. That's my way, sir; and there are many victories worse than a defeat.

Opposition may become sweet to a man when he has christened it persecution.

I'm not denying that women are foolish. God Almighty made them to match men.

In *Westminster Review*, January 1857
On Edward Young, poet

A sort of cross between a sycophant and a psalmist.

On Adam Bede

He was like a cock who thought the sun had risen to hear him crow.

In *Impressions of Theophrastus Such*

Blessed is the man who, having nothing to say, abstains from giving in words evidence of the fact.

QUEEN ELIZABETH I (1533–1603)

Anger makes dull men witty, but it keeps them poor.

NORA EPHRON (*b.* 1941)
American journalist
Quoted in *Esquire*, 1970

How can you be angry at someone who's got your number?

EDNA FERBER (1885–1968)
American writer and playwright
On Alexander Woollcott

This New Jersey Nero who mistakes his pinafore for a toga.

FENELLA FIELDING (*b.* 1934)
Anglo-Rumanian actress
'Sayings of the Week' (*Observer*)

Men are people, just like women.

RACHAEL HEYHOE-FLINT
Captain of England's women's cricket team
'Sayings of the Week' (*Observer*)

We have nothing against men cricketers. Some of them are quite nice people, even though they don't win as often as we do.

ZELDA FITZGERALD (1900–1948)
In her review of *The Beautiful and Damned*, quoted in Nancy Mitford's *Zelda Fitzgerald*

In fact, Mr Fitzgerald – I believe that is how he spells his name – seems to believe that plagiarism begins at home.

JUANA FRANCES
Spanish artist

Man is trampled by the same forces he has created.

ELLEN FRANKFORT
American feminist

With almost all doctors, population experts, and drug manufacturers male, is it really a surprise that oral contraceptives were designed for women to take and men to promote?

PAULINE FREDERICK (1883–1938)
American actress

When a man gets up to speak, people listen, then look. When a woman gets up, people *look*; then, if they like what they see, they listen.

BETTY FRIEDAN (*b.* 1921)
American feminist

Man is not the enemy here, but the fellow victim. The real enemy is women's denigration of themselves.

BARBARA FUCA

A Mafia wife can hate her husband, but something she never does is divorce him while he is in jail.

ELIZABETH GASKELL (1810–1865)
British writer
In *Cranford*

A man . . . is *so* in the way in the house.

JEAN GIRAUDOUX (1882–1944)
French writer
In *Tiger at the Gates*

You know women as well as I do. They are only willing when you compel them, but after that they're as enthusiastic as you are.

GERMAINE GREER (*b.* 1939)
Australian feminist
In *The Female Eunuch*

It is known that a father is necessary, but not known how to identify him, except negatively.

Quoted in the *Observer*, 1979

I love men like some people like good food or wine.

Men can allow themselves to run to seed in the most appalling fashion. Women tolerate it because they think they are not entitled to ask for anything more.

MOLLY HASKELL
Writer
In *From Reverence to Rape*

Of all the silent comedians, Laurel and Hardy are perhaps most threatening to women, as they combine the physical ruination with misogyny . . . With their disaster-prone bodies and their exclusive relationship that not only shuts out women but questions their very necessity, they constitute a two-man wrecking team of female – that is, civilized and bourgeois – society.

HEDDA HOPPER (1890–1966)
American theatre columnist
On Harry Cohn

You had to stay in line to hate him.

MILLIE JACKSON
American soul singer

I think women who say they're not dependent on men are liars. I don't know any lady plumbers.

ERICA JONG (*b.* 1942)
American writer

You see an awful lot of smart guys with dumb women, but you hardly ever see a smart woman with a dumb guy.

PAULINE KAEL
American theatre critic
On Cecil B. de Mille

He made small-minded pictures on a big scale.

SALLY KEMPTON (*b.* 1943)
American journalist

It is hard to fight an enemy who has outposts in your head.

Men are brought up to command, women to seduce. To admit the necessity of seduction is to admit that one has not the strength to command.

MARY KINDER (*circa* 1920s)
A mistress of John Dillinger
In Robert Cromie's *Dillinger, A Short and Violent Life*

Johnnie's just an ordinary fellow. Of course he goes out and holds up banks and things, but he's really just like any other fellow, aside from that.

FRIEDA LAWRENCE
Writer and wife of D. H. Lawrence
In *Not I, but the Wind*

Lawrence was so direct, such a real puritan! He hated any *haut-goût* or lewdness. Fine underclothing and all the apparatus of the seducing sort were just stupid to him . . . Passionate people don't need tricks.

JENNIE LEE
British politician and widow of Aneurin Bevan
In Michael Foot's *Aneurin Bevan*

Nye was born old and died young.

ROSAMUND LEHMANN (*b.* 1905)
British novelist
In John Pearson's *Life of Ian Fleming*

The trouble with Ian is that he gets off with women because he can't get on with them.

FLORENCE BECKER LENNON
In *Lewis Carroll*

Carroll's superiority over Barrie is that his mawkish writings are his dull ones – he never succeeds in making sentimentality seductive.

Barrie struck twelve once – with *Peter Pan* – a subtly unwholesome sweetmeat, like most of his books.

LADY LEWISHAM (now Countess Spencer) (*b.* 1929)
British aristocrat

Nothing is more debasing for a real man than a plastic apron.

MARY WILSON LITTLE
American writer

If a man is only a little lower than the angels, the angels should reform.

GINA LOLLOBRIGIDA (*b.* 1927)
Italian film star
Quoted in the *Observer*, 1956

Glamour is when a man knows a woman is a woman.

ANITA LOOS (*b.* 1893)
American novelist
In *Gentlemen Prefer Blondes*

So this gentleman said a girl with brains ought to do something else with them besides think.

Kissing your hand may make you feel very, very good but a diamond and sapphire bracelet lasts for ever.

CLARE BOOTHE LUCE (*b.* 1903)
American writer and diplomat

There's nothing like a good dose of another woman to make a man appreciate his wife.

A man's home may seem to be his castle on the outside; inside it is more often his nursery.

Technological man can't believe in anything that can't be measured, taped, put in a computer.

LADY LYTTON
In Christopher Hassall's *Edward Marsh*
On Winston Churchill

The first time you meet Winston you see all his faults, and the rest of your life you spend in discovering his virtues!

MARY MCCARTHY (*b.* 1912)
American writer
In *On The Contrary*

When an American heiress wants to buy a man, she at once crosses the Atlantic.

PHYLLIS MCGINLEY (*b.* 1905)
Canadian writer
On 'The Honour of being a Woman'

Women are not men's equals in anything except responsibility. We are not their inferiors, either, or even their superiors. We are quite simply different races.

MARY MCGRORY (*b.* 1918)
American journalist

Richard Nixon was like a kamikaze pilot who kept apologizing for the attack.

SHIRLEY MACLAINE (*b.* 1934)
American actress
On Jimmy Carter

He says his lust is in his heart. I hope it's a little lower.

KATHERINE MANSFIELD (1890–1923)
New Zealand-born writer

E. M. Forster never gets any further than warming the teapot. He's a rare fine hand at that. Feel this teapot. Is it not beautifully warm? Yes, but there ain't going to be no tea.

ANN-MARGRET (*b.* 1941)
Swedish-American film star

A man who is honest with himself wants a woman to be soft and feminine, careful of what she's saying and talk like a man.

MARGARET MEAD (1901–1978)
American anthropologist

Throughout history, females have picked providers for males. Males pick anything.

Women want mediocre men, and men are working hard to be as mediocre as possible.

SUSAN MITCHELL
In O. St John Gogarty's *As I Was Going Down Sackville Street*

Some men kiss and do not tell, some kiss and tell; but George Moore told and did not kiss.

MARILYN MONROE (1926–1962)
American film star

A strong man doesn't have to be dominant toward a woman. He doesn't match his strength against a woman weak with love for him. He matches it against the world.

Men are always ready to respect anything that bores them.

HANNAH MORE (1745–1835)
English poet

In men this blunder still you find,
All think their little set mankind.

LADY MORGAN
On George Canning

His absorbing idea was to be the political Atlas of England, to raise her on his shoulders.

LADY OTTOLINE MORRELL (1873–1938)
British society hostess and patron
In Robert Gathorne-Hardy's *Ottoline at Garsington*
On Bertrand Russell

He only feels life through his brain, or through sex, and there is a gulf between these two separate departments.

KITTY MUGGERIDGE
On David Frost

Frost has risen without trace.

CAROLINA OLIPHANT (Lady Nairne) (1766–1845)

Sweet's the laverock's note and lang,
Lilting wildly up the glen;

But aye to me he sings ae sang,
Will ye no come back again?

YOKO ONO (*b.* 1933)
Japanese-born artist

Men have an unusual talent for making a bore out of everything they touch.

Somebody told me that I don't make small talk and that's why men hate me.

DOROTHY PARKER (1895–1967)
American writer and wit

I require only three things of a man. He must be handsome, ruthless, and stupid.

In *One Perfect Rose*

Why is it no one ever sent me yet
One perfect limousine, do you suppose?
Ah no, it's always just my luck to get
One perfect rose.

In *Sunset Gun*

When I admit neglect of Gissing,
They say I don't know what I'm missing,
Until their arguments are subtler,
I think I'll stick to Samuel Butler.

In *Enough Rope*

Woman wants monogamy;
Man delights in novelty.

Quoted in her obituary, *New York Times*, 8 June 1967

Woman's life must be wrapped up in a man, and the cleverest woman on earth is the biggest fool with a man.

RUTH STAFFORD PEALE

A man's job, basically, is to tame this world: a wife's job is to control herself – and indirectly her husband.

MRS PABLO PICASSO
On Pablo Picasso

If my husband would ever meet a woman on the streets who looked like the women in his paintings, he would fall over in a dead faint.

MARY PICKFORD (1893–1979)
American actress
On her former husband, Douglas Fairbanks

Douglas had always faced a situation the only way he knew how, by running away from it.

HESTER PIOZZI (Mrs Thrale) (1741–1821)
British poet
On Dr Samuel Johnson

He loved the poor as I never yet saw any one else do, with an earnest desire to make them happy. What signifies, says someone, giving halfpence to common beggars? They only lay it out in gin and tobacco. 'And why should they be denied such sweeteners of their existence?' says Johnson. 'It is surely very savage to refuse them every possible avenue to pleasure, reckoned too coarse for our own acceptance . . .'

DIANA QUICK (*b.* 1946)
British actress

If there are women who can help themselves, who go to work *and* run the home, then what are men for?

JANE BRYANT QUINN
Quoted in *Newsweek*, 9 October 1978

Lawyers are . . . operators of the toll bridge across which anyone in search of justice must pass.

AGNES REPPLIER (1858–1950)
American essayist
Points of View ('A Plea for Humour')

If a man be discreet enough to take to hard drinking in his youth, before his general emptiness is ascertained, his friends invariably credit him with a host of shining qualities which, we are given to understand, lie balked and frustrated by his one unfortunate weakness.

In *Compromises* ('The Luxury of Conversation')

A man who listens because he has nothing to say can hardly be a source of inspiration. The only listening that counts is that of the talker who alternately absorbs and expresses ideas.

NAN ROBERTSON

Ever since Eve gave Adam the apple, there has been a misunderstanding between the sexes about gifts.

HELEN ROWLAND (1875–1950)

American journalist

The only original thing about some men is original sin.

Failing to be there when a man wants her is a woman's greatest sin, except to be there when he doesn't want her.

There are only two kinds of men – the dead and the deadly.

CLAIRE RUTH

Widow of Babe Ruth, baseball player

Quoted in *New York Times*, 12 August 1973

I don't even have an autographed ball. You don't ask your husband for an autographed ball. He'd probably think you were nuts.

FRANÇOISE SAGAN (*b.* 1936)

French novelist

I like men to behave like men . . . strong and childish.

KATHIE SARACHILD

American feminist

The only problem with women is men.

ADELA ROGERS ST JOHN (*b.* 1894)
American writer
On Clark Gable

Gable. The King. An exaggeration of a man.

On Fatty Arbuckle

. . . My father had said at once that, though he was innocent, beyond question he would be publicly castigated because it was repulsive to think of a fat man in the role of a rapist.

BARBARA SEAMAN
Quoted in *New York Post*, 28 September 1973

Delivering a baby is the ultimate male ego trip.

MADAME DE SÉVIGNÉ (1626–1692)
French writer

I fear nothing so much as a man who is witty all day long.

MARY SHELLEY (1797–1851)
British writer
In a letter to John Murray, 19 January 1830

Our Lord Byron – the fascinating – faulty – childish – philosophical being – daring the world – docile to a private circle – impetuous and indolent – gloomy and yet more gay than any other.

DAME EDITH SITWELL (1887–1964)
British poet
On Wyndham Lewis

Mr Lewis's pictures appeared, as a very great painter said to me, to have been painted by a mailed fist in a cotton glove.

PATTI SMITH (*b.* 1946)
American rock singer

I don't like to see boys wearing make-up.

SUSAN SONTAG (*b.* 1933)
American writer
In *Notes on Camp*

What is most beautiful in virile men is something feminine; what is most beautiful in feminine women is something masculine.

MURIEL SPARK (*b.* 1918)
British novelist

Do you think it pleases a man when he looks into a woman's eyes and sees a reflection of the British Museum Reading Room?

MADAM DE STAËL (1766–1817)
French writer

The more I see of men, the more I like dogs.

ELIZABETH CADY STANTON (1815–1902)
American suffragette

I found nothing grand in the history of the Jews nor in the morals inculcated in the Pentateuch. I know of no other books that so fully teach the subjection and degradation of women.

KOO STARK (*b.* 1955)
British actress

I like responsible men, men that are used to responsibilities, men that are father figures.

CHRISTINA STEAD (*b.* 1902)
Australian-born novelist

A self-made man is one who believes in luck and sends his son to Oxford.

If all the rich men in the world divided up their money amongst themselves, there wouldn't be enough to go round.

GERTRUDE STEIN (1874–1946)
American writer
On Ezra Pound

A village explainer, excellent if you were a village, but if you were not, not.

CAITLIN THOMAS
Widow of Dylan Thomas
Quoted in Andrew Sinclair's *Dylan Thomas, Poet of His People*

He was never his proper self till there was something wrong with him; and, if there was a danger of him becoming 'whole', which was very remote, he would crack another of his chicken bones, without delay, and wander happily round in his sling, piling up plates with cucumber, pickled onions, tins of cod's roe, boiled sweets; to push into his mouth with an unseeing hand, as they came, while he went on solidly reading his trash.

On her husband's attitude to women

A woman's place . . . is in the bed or at the sink, and the extent of her travels should be from one to the other and back.

IRENE THOMAS (*b.* 1929)
British broadcaster

It should be a very happy marriage – they are both so much in love with *him*.

HENRIETTA TIARKS (*b.* 1940)
British aristocrat

A gentleman is a patient wolf.

FRANCES TROLLOPE (1780–1863)
British writer

I hardly know any annoyance so deeply repugnant to English feelings, as the incessant remorseless spitting of Americans.

I never saw an American man walk or stand well; they are nearly all hollow-chested and round-shouldered.

I suppose there is less alms-giving in America than in any other Christian country on the face of the globe. It is not in the temper of the people either to give or to receive.

MARGARET TRUDEAU (*b.* 1949)
Former wife of Canadian Prime Minister

I'm officially resigning as the prime minister's wife.

AMANDA VAIL
In *Love Me Little*

Sometimes I think if there was a third sex men wouldn't get so much as a glance from me.

LUPE VELEZ (1908–1944)
Mexican film star

The first time you buy a house you see how pretty the paint is and buy it. The second time you look to see if the basement has termites. It's the same with men.

EUGENE FITCH WARE
In *The Last Laugh*

When I am dead you'll find it hard,
  Said he,
To ever find another man
  Like me.

What makes you think, as I suppose
  You do,
I'd ever want another man
  Like you?

KATHARINE WHITEHORN
British journalist
On 'Husband Swapping' (*Observer*)

The Life and Soul, the man who will never go home while there is one man, woman or glass of anything not yet drunk.

And what would happen to my illusion that I am a force for

order in the home if I wasn't married to the only man north of the Tiber who is even untidier than I am?

ANNA WICKHAM (*b.* 1883)
Australian-born poet
In *The Affinity*

The true male never yet walked
Who liked to listen when his mate talked.

From a wealth of living I have proved
I must be silent, if I would be loved.

RAQUEL WELCH (*b.* 1940)
American actress
Quoted in *The Sunday Times*

There aren't any hard women, just soft men.

VITA SACKVILLE-WEST (1892–1962)
British poet
In a letter to Harold Nicolson, her husband, 9 December 1959

It always makes me cross when Max [Beerbohm] is called 'The Incomparable Max'. He is not incomparable at all, and in fact compares very poorly with Harold Nicolson, as a stylist, as a wit, and an observer of human nature. He is a shallow, affected, self-conscious fribble – so there.

MAE WEST (1892–1980)
American film star

He's the kind of man who picks his friends – to pieces.

A man in the house is worth two in the street.

Give a man a free hand and he'll run it all over you.

DAME REBECCA WEST (1892–1983)
British novelist

He is every other inch a gentleman.

RUTH WESTON
American actress

A fox is a wolf who sends flowers.

CHARLOTTE WHITTON (1896–1975)
Former mayor of Ottaway

Whatever women do they must do twice as well as men to be thought half as good. Luckily, this is not difficult.

CONSTANCE WILDE (*née* Lloyd)
Wife of Oscar Wilde
In a letter to her brother, 26 March 1897
On her husband

I think his fate is rather like Humpty Dumpty's, quite as tragic and quite as impossible to put right.

WOMEN'S LIBERATION SLOGAN
Australia, 1975

If you catch a man, throw him back.

VIRGINIA WOOLF (1882–1941)
British writer

Women have served all these centuries as looking glasses possessing the . . . power of reflecting the figure of man at twice its natural size.

In *A Room of One's Own*

The fact is that neither Mr Galsworthy nor Mr Kipling has a spark of the woman in him. Thus all their qualities seem to a woman, if one may generalize, crude and immature. They lack suggestive power. And when a book lacks suggestive power, however hard it hits the surface of the mind, it cannot penetrate within.

PATRICIA YOUNG
On Sir Thomas Beecham

At a dinner given in honour of his seventieth birthday, when messages of congratulation from great musicians all over the world were being read out, Sir Thomas was heard to murmur, 'What, nothing from Mozart?'

SULTANA ZORAYA
Former wife of the late Shah of Persia

Coward: a man in whom the instinct of self-preservation acts normally.

LOVE

SHANA ALEXANDER
American journalist and broadcaster
In *The Feminine Eye*

The mark of a true crush (whether the object is man, woman or city) is that you fall in love first and grope for reasons afterward.

HENRI FRÉDÉRIC AMIEL (1821–1881)
Swiss writer

Women wish to be loved without a why or a wherefore; not because they are pretty, or good, or well-bred, or graceful, or intelligent, but because they are themselves.

MARGARET ANDERSON (1891–1973)
American author

In real love you want the other person's good. In romantic love you want the other person.

HANNAH ARENDT (1906–1975)
German-American political philosopher

Love, in distinction from friendship, is killed, or rather extinguished, the moment it is displayed in public.

ARLETTY (Alette-Léonie Bathiat) (*b.* 1898)
French actress

Etre loin de Paris, pour moi c'est l'exil.

JANE AUSTEN (1775–1817)
British novelist

One does not love a place the less for having suffered in it.

BRIGITTE BARDOT (*b.* 1933)
French actress
'Sayings of the Week' (*Observer*, 29 December 1968)

It's better to be unfaithful than faithful without wanting to be.

INGRID BERGMAN (1915–1982)
Swedish actress
In the film *Casablanca*

Play it once, Sam, for old time's sake. (As Time Goes By)

ISAAC BICKERSTAFFE (*circa* 1735–1812)
British playwright

We all love a pretty girl – under the rose.

ELIZABETH BOWEN (1899–1973)
Anglo-Irish writer
In *The Death of the Heart*

The wish to lead out one's lover must be a tribal feeling: the wish to be seen as loved is part of one's self-respect.

In *The House in Paris*

Jealousy is no more than feeling alone against smiling enemies.

RITA MAE BROWN (*b.* 1944)
American writer

To love without role, without power plays, is revolution.

ELIZABETH BARRETT BROWNING (1806–1861)
British poet
In *Aurora Leigh*

Whoso loves
Believes the impossible.

In *Sonnets from the Portuguese*

If thou must love me, let it be for naught
Except for love's sake only.

PEARL S. BUCK (1892–1973)
American novelist
In *To My Daughters, With Love*

Love dies only when growth stops.

To serve is beautiful, but only if it is done with joy and a whole heart and a free mind.

ROBERT BURNS (1759–1796)
Scottish poet
In *Ae Fond Kiss*

But to see her was to love her,
Love but her, and love for ever.

LORD BYRON (1788–1824)
British poet
In *Don Juan*

Sweet is revenge – especially to women.

In her first passion woman loves her love
In all the others all she loves is love.

MARIA CALLAS (1923–1977)
Greek-born opera singer

Love is so much better when you are not married.

JULIA CARNEY (1823–1908)

Little deeds of kindness, little words of love,
Help to make earth happy, like the heaven above.

BARBARA CARTLAND (*b.* 1904)
British novelist
'Sayings of the Week' (*Observer*)

There's no substitute for moonlight and kissing.

CATULLUS (87–54? BC)

But what a woman says to her desirous lover should be written in wind and swift-flowing water.

CHER (*b.* 1946)
American singer
Quoted in *Playboy*, 1975

Romance and work are great diversions to keep you from dealing with yourself.

SAMUEL T. COLERIDGE (1772–1834)
British poet
In *Table Talk*

The man's desire is for the woman; but the woman's desire is rarely other than for the desire of the man.

COLETTE (Sidonie-Gabrielle) (1873–1954)
French writer
In *Earthly Paradise*

Jealousy is not at all low, but it catches us humbled and bowed down, at first sight.

The following note, signed Sidonie Colette, *née* Landoy, was written by Colette to the husband of her daughter, a year before Colette died. (Quoted in Robert Dougall's *Now For the Good News*)

Monsieur,

You ask me to come and spend a week with you, which means I would be near my daughter, whom I adore. You who live with her, well know how rarely I see her, how much her presence delights me, and I am touched that you should ask me to come and see her.

All the same I am not going to accept your kind invitation, for the time being at any rate. The reason is that my pink cactus is probably going to flower. It is a very rare plant I've been given, and I'm told that in our climate it flowers only once every four years. Now, I am already a very old woman; and if I went away when my pink cactus was going to flower, I am certain I shouldn't see it flower again.

CHARLES CALEB COLTON (1780–1832)
British clergyman and writer
In *Lacon*

Women generally consider consequences in love, seldom in resentment.

WILLIAM CONGREVE (1670–1729)
British playwright
In *The Mourning Bride*

Heaven has no rage like love to hatred turned,
Nor hell a fury, like a woman scorned.

CYRIL CONNOLLY (1903–1974)
British critic
In *The Unquiet Grave*

There is no fury like a woman searching for a new lover.

FRANCES CORNFORD
British writer
In *To a Fat Lady Seen from a Train*

O why do you walk through the fields in gloves,
Missing so much and so much?
O fat white woman whom nobody loves.

JOHN DONNE (1572–1631)
British poet and cleric

Come live with me, and be my love,
And we will some new pleasures prove.

MARLENE DIETRICH (*b.* 1901)
German actress

Grumbling is the death of love.

MAUREEN DUFFY (*b.* 1933)
British writer
In *Wounds*

Love is the only effective counter to death.

GEORGE ELIOT (Marian Evans) (1819–1880)
British novelist

It is a common enough case, that of a man being suddenly captivated by a woman nearly the opposite of his ideal.

GEORGE FARQUHAR (1678–1707)
Irish dramatist
In *The Beaux' Stratagem*

How a little love and good company improves a woman!

MARGARET FULLER (1810–1850)
American writer and critic

It seems that it is madder never to abandon one's self than often to be infatuated; better to be wounded, a captive and a slave, than always to walk in armour.

JOHN GAY (1685–1732)
British poet
In *Dione*

A woman's friendship ever ends in love.

MARGARET GILMAN

If love makes the world go round
Why are we going to outer space?

HERMIONE GINGOLD (*b.* 1897)
British actress
'Sayings of the Week' (*Observer*)
On announcing her engagement to an antique dealer at the age of 74

He loves antiques and I think that's why he fell for me.

ROBERT GRAVES (*b.* 1895)
British poet

For a woman to have a liaison is almost always pardonable, and occasionally, when the lover chosen is sufficiently distinguished, even admirable; but in love as in sport, the amateur status must be strictly maintained.

DORA GREENWELL (1821–1882)
In *Home*

A world of care without,
A world of strife shut out,
A world of love shut in.

GERMAINE GREER (*b.* 1939)
Australian feminist
In *The Female Eunuch*

Love is . . . the drug which makes sexuality palatable in popular mythology.

Love, love, love – all the wretched cant of it, masking egotism, lust, masochism, fantasy under a mythology of sentimental postures, a welter of self-induced miseries and joys, blinding and masking the essential personalities in the frozen gestures of courtship, in the kissing and the dating and the desire, the compliments and the quarrels which vivify its barrenness.

MRS DE GREY
In *Fragments on Women*

Affection is the natural element of woman; once yielded to, it becomes interwoven in her frame, forms a part of every thought and every feeling, and is not a chance ingredient in the cup of happiness, but becomes the draught itself. Men have many things to do and to think of, which are unconnected with each other; but women's feelings are more exclusive. There is no pursuit, how simple soever in appearance; no contemplation, however sublime in fact, with which they do not continue to blend the recollection of a beloved object . . . It is their thoughts alone which give them activity and life, for their actions are circumscribed; yet how often is there more to relate in their apparently monotonous existence than in ours!

DEBBIE HARRY (*b.* 1941)
American rock singer

I wouldn't mind being a mom. I already am a housewife.

Everybody keeps reading in the papers that we live in this luxury penthouse – but it's just a crummy apartment. The building is falling apart: you can see the peeling paint, the leaking roof and the mould on the walls . . . but we love it! It's home!

JOHN HAY (1838–1905)
American statesman and writer

Wisely a woman prefers to a lover a man who neglects her. This one may love her some day, some day the lover will not.

HELEN HAYES (*b.* 1900)
American actress

The story of a love is not important – what is important is that one is capable of love.

There is only one terminal dignity – love.

LILLIAN HELLMAN (*b.* 1907)
American playwright

Everybody's mother still cares.

KATHARINE HEPBURN (*b.* 1909)
American actress

Being a housewife and a mother is the biggest job in the world, but if it doesn't interest you, don't do it . . . I would have made a terrible parent. The first time my child didn't do what I wanted, I'd kill him.

AMY JOHNSON (1903–1941)
British solo flyer

On the break-up of her marriage to Jim Mollison

Jim of course has been my undoing, but I would do just the same if I had the chance over again. Women are fools enough to love the men who hurt them most . . . I am still very much in love with Jim but am as unhappy with him as away from him . . .

HELEN KELLER (1880–1968)
Writer and lecturer (born deaf and blind)
In *My Religion*

As selfishness and complaint pervert and cloud the mind, so love with its joys clears and sharpens the vision.

MARGHANITA LASKI
British historian and broadcaster
In *Everyday Ecstasy*

The most usual result of an ecstasy or a response experience is probably nothing beyond a transitory feeling of betterment. But of more substantial results, the most common is what it is reasonable to call falling in love: that is, the creation for the time being, of a new focus of obsessive interest.

EMMA LAZARUS (1849–1887)
American poet
In *Sonnet to the Statue of Liberty*

Give me your tired, your poor,
Your huddled masses yearning to breathe free,
The wretched refuse of your teeming shore,
Send those, the homeless, tempest-tost to me.
I lift my lamp beside the golden door!

ANNE MORROW LINDBERGH (*b.* 1906)
American writer
In *The Unicorn and Other Poems* ('Even')

Him that I love, I wish to be
Free –
Even from me.

SOPHIE IRENE LOEB (1876–1929)
American social reformer

Platonic friendship: the interval between the introduction and the first kiss.

AMELIA LOWELL (1874–1925)
American poet
In *A Shard of Silence* ('Thorn Piece')

A place is nothing, not even space,
Unless at its heart a figure stands.

SHIRLEY MACLAINE (*b.* 1934)
American actress

The pain of leaving those you grow to love is only the prelude to an understanding of yourself and others.

PHYLLIS MCGINLEY (*b.* 1905)
Canadian writer
In *The Province of the Heart* ('In Defense of Sin')

A girl (and perhaps the same thing applies to a boy) would find life less broken apart after a misguided love affair if she could feel that she had been sinful rather than a fool.

JOYCE MCKINNEY
'Sayings of the Week' (*Observer*)

I loved Kirk so much I would have ski-ed down Mount Everest in the nude with a carnation up my nose.

ANNA MAGNANI (1908–1973)
Italian actress
In *The Egotists*

Great passions don't exist – they are liar's fantasies. What do exist are little loves that may last for a short or longer while.

W. SOMERSET MAUGHAM (1874–1965)
British novelist
In *Lady Frederick*

Women's hearts are like old china, none the worse for a break or two.

When a man's in love, he at once makes a pedestal of the Ten Commandments and stands on the top of them with his arms akimbo. When a woman's in love she doesn't care two straws for Thou Shalt and Thou Shalt Not.

In *The Summing Up*

It takes two to make a love affair and a man's meat is too often a woman's poison.

In *The Moon and Sixpence*

Because women can do nothing except love, they've given it a ridiculous importance.

MARGARET MEAD (1901–1978)
American anthropologist
In a speech to National Council of Women, New York City, 16 April 1975

Having someone wonder where you are when you don't come home at night is a very old human need.

BETTE MIDLER (*b.* 1945)
American entertainer

Unrequited love is a subject very near and dear to my heart. I love that shit. I love to bare my breast.

EDNA ST VINCENT MILLAY (1892–1950)
American poet
In *To the Not Impossible Him*

The fabric of my faithful love
No power shall dim or ravel
Whilst I stay here, – but oh, my dear,
If I should ever travel!

It's not love's going hurts my days
But that it went in little ways.

In *Theme and Variations*

I have loved badly, loved the great
Too soon, withdrawn my words too late;
And eaten in an echoing hall
Alone and from a chipped plate
The words that I withdrew too late.

JEAN BAPTISTE MOLIÈRE (1622–1673)
French playwright
In *The Sicilian*

To inspire love is a woman's greatest ambition, believe me. It's the one thing women care about and there's no woman so proud that she doesn't rejoice at heart in her conquests.

LADY MARY WORTLEY MONTAGU (1689–1762)
British writer
On Lord Lyttelton's advice

Be plain in dress, and sober in your diet;
In short, my deary! kiss me, and be quiet.

MARABEL MORGAN

Love never makes demands. Love is unconditional acceptance of him and his feelings.

IRIS MURDOCH (*b.* 1919)
British philosopher and novelist

Falling out of love is very enlightening, for a short while you see the world with new eyes.

Love . . . is the extremely difficult realisation that something other than oneself is real.

GEORGE JEAN NATHAN (1882–1958)
American critic

Love is the emotion that a woman feels always for a poodle dog and sometimes for a man.

CHRISTINA ONASSIS (*b.* 1950)
Daughter of Aristotle Onassis

My most fervent wish is that I shall meet a man who loves me for myself and not for my money.

OVID (43 BC–AD 17)
Latin poet
In *The Art of Love*

Whether a pretty woman grants or withholds her favours, she always likes to be asked for them.

What they [women] like to give, they love to be robbed of.

I hate a woman who offers herself because she ought to do so, and, cold and dry, thinks of her sewing when she's making love.

Women can always be caught; that's the first rule of the game.

Many women long for what eludes them, and like not what is offered them.

MR JUSTICE PARK (*b.* 1910)
British judge
'Sayings of the Week' (*Observer*)

I do not see why any wife should be expected to go back to a husband who said he did not love her.

DOROTHY PARKER (1893–1967)
American writer and wit
In *Enough Rope* ('Ballade of Great Weariness')

Scratch a lover, and find a foe!

In *Enough Rope* ('Indian Summer')

Now I know the things I know,
And do the things I do,
And if you do not like me so,
To hell, my love, with you!

In *Death and Taxes* ('Summary')

Every love's the love before
In a duller dress.

ARUNDEL PENRUDDOCK

The following letter of farewell was written to her husband,

John Penruddock, a Royalist, who was beheaded at Exeter, 3 May 1655. (Quoted by Robert Dougall in *Now for the Good News*.)

My dear Heart,

My sad parting was so far from making me forget you, that I scarce thought upon myself since, but wholly upon you. Those dear embraces which I yet feel, and shall never lose, being the faithful testimonies of an indulgent husband, have charmed my soul to such a reverence of your remembrance, that were it possible, I would, with my own blood, cement your dead limbs to live again . . . Oh! my dear, you must now pardon my passion, this being my last . . . that ever you will receive from me; and know, that until the last minute that I can imagine you shall live, I shall sacrifice the prayers of a Christian and the groans of an afflicted wife . . .

I would fain discourse longer with you, but dare not; passion begins to drown my reason, and will rob me of my devoirs, which is all I have left to serve you. Adieu, therefore, ten thousand times, my dearest dear; and since I must never see you more, take this prayer – May your faith be so strengthened that your constancy may continue; and then I know Heaven will receive you; whither grief and love will in a short time (I hope) translate,

My dear, Your sad, but constant wife, even to love your ashes when dead,

Arundel Penruddock.

HESTER LYNCH PIOZZI (Mrs Thrale) (1741–1821)
British writer

In a letter to Fanny Burney, 1781

'Tis never for their wisdom that one loves the wisest, or for their wit that one loves the wittiest: 'tis for benevolence and virtue and honest fondness one loves people.

PLUTARCH (*circa* AD 46–120)
Greek historian and biographer

It is a high distinction for a homely woman to be loved for her character rather than for beauty.

KATHARINE ANNE PORTER (1890–1980)
American writer

Love is purely a creation of the human imagination . . . the most important example of how the imagination continually outruns the creature it inhabits.

MARCEL PROUST (1871–1922)
French novelist

A woman we love rarely satisfies all our needs, and we deceive her with a woman whom we do not love.

ADRIENNE RICH (*b.* 1929)
American poet and feminist

I'd call it love if love
didn't take so many years
but lust too is a jewel.

FRANÇOIS SAGAN (*b.* 1936)
French novelist
In *La Chamade*

To jealousy, nothing is more frightful than laughter.

Every little girl knows about love. It is only her capacity to suffer because of it that increases.

J. D. SALINGER (*b.* 1919)
American novelist
In *The Catcher in the Rye*

I was about half in love with her by the time we sat down. That's the thing about girls. Every time they do something pretty, even if they're not much to look at, or even if they're sort of stupid, you fall half in love with them, and then you never know *where* the hell you are.

PRINCESS CAROLYNE JEANNE ELISABETH VON SAYNWITTGENSTEIN
Russian lover of Franz Liszt
In a letter to Liszt, *circa* 1847

I kiss your hands and kneel before you, prostrating my forehead to your feet to assure you that my whole mind, all the breadth of my spirit, all my heart exist only to love you. I adore you, dear Masterpiece of God – so beautiful, so perfect, so made to be cherished, adored and loved to death and madness.

GEORGE BERNARD SHAW (1856–1950)
Irish playwright
In *The Philanderer*

The fickleness of the women I love is only equalled by the infernal constancy of the women who love me.

DINAH SHORE
American actress

Trouble is a part of your life, and if you don't share it, you don't give the person who loves you a chance to love you enough.

CORNELIA OTIS SKINNER (1901–1979)
American actress

One learns in life to keep silent and draw one's own confusions.

GRACE SLICK (*b.* 1939)
American rock singer

People, let's not be laying our bodies on each other unless we intend love.

GODFREY SMITH
British journalist
In his introduction to *A World of Love*

Women, trapped by their biological imperatives and

systematically deprived of their political and economic rights over the centuries, have been bamboozled into accepting the emotional solace of romantic love instead. From the rise of the troubadors, they have been put on a pedestal: a very good position, as one cynic observed, for looking up their skirts. Come to think of it, there is not much room for anything on a pedestal: travel, adventure, change, experiment.

. . . Yet the yearning for romance flourishes and is nourished by the booming house of Mills and Boon. Miss Barbara Cartland has become a millionaire simply because women want to go on being bamboozled . . .

If a personal instance of this new cool style [of boy-girl relationships] may be forgiven, one of my daughters, in Oxford for her entrance examination, left a loving message for a boyfriend due to take a similar hurdle at another college a few days later. It read, in its entirety: 'Sock it to them, shitface.'

MADAME DE STAËL (1766–1817)
French writer

We cease loving ourselves if no one loves us.

HENRI BEYLE DE STENDHAL (1783–1842)
French writer
In *On Love*

If one is sure of a woman's love one asks one's self if she is more or less beautiful; if one is in doubt as to her feelings one has no time to think of her appearance.

SARA TEASDALE (1884–1933)
American poet
In *Days' Ending*

Take love when love is given,
But never think to find it
A sure escape from sorrow
Or a complete repose.

In *The Kiss*

Though I know he loves me,
Tonight my heart is sad;
His kiss was not so wonderful
As all the dreams I had.

In *New Love and Old*

Old love, old love,
How can I be true?
Shall I be faithless to myself
Or to you?

IRENE THOMAS (*b.* 1929)
British broadcaster and quiz expert

After so many years I can honestly say that . . . we can answer each other's questions halfway through. (Where's the . . .? Right-hand kitchen cupboard, top shelf.) I am continually amused and delighted by my husband's company. Infuriating he often is – boring never.

MARGARET TRUDEAU (*b.* 1948)
Former wife of Canadian Prime Minister

I can't be a rose in any man's lapel.

SIMONE WEIL (1909–1943)
French philosopher

Love is not consolation, it is light.

H. G. WELLS (1866–1946)
British novelist and sociologist
In *Bealby*

Miss Madeleine Philips was making it very manifest to Captain Douglas that she herself was a career; that a lover with any other career in view need not – as the advertisements say – apply.

EUDORA WELTY (*b.* 1909)
American writer

Out of love you can speak with straight fury.

MAE WEST (1892–1980)
American film star

I never loved another person the way I loved myself.

The best way to hold a man is in your arms.

Love conquers all things except poverty and toothache.

Just a little more loving and a lot less fighting and the world would be all right.

TOYAH WILLCOX (*b.* 1958)
British actress and rock singer

With music I'm lying there naked, saying 'This is me', saying what I feel, having an affair with every member of the audience. It's an important form of communication to me.

THE DUCHESS OF WINDSOR (*b.* 1896)
'Sayings of the Week' (*Observer*, 28 April 1974)

Today women give up too easily. I think they should play harder to get.

THYRA SAMTER WINSLOW (1903–1961)
American writer

Platonic love is love from the neck up.

SHELLEY WINTERS (*b.* 1922)
American actress

Security is when I'm very much in love with somebody extraordinary who loves me back.

SEX

BELLA ABZUG (*b.* 1920)
American politician

Abortion doesn't belong in the political arena. It's a private right, like many other rights concerning the family.

POLLY ADLER (1900–1962)
American madam

Too many cooks spoil the brothel.

LISA ALTHER (*b.* 1944)
American writer
In *Kinflicks*

People knew a man by the company he kept, but they generally knew a woman by the man who kept her.

ANONYMOUS
On the Profumo affair

What have you done? cried Christine,
You've wrecked the whole party machine.
To lie in the nude may be rude,
But to lie in the House is obscene.

ANONYMOUS

Little nips of whisky, little drops of gin,
Make a lady wonder where on earth she's bin.

ANONYMOUS
In Seymour Hicks' *Vintage Years*

When Lady Jane became a tart,
It almost broke her father's heart.
But blood is blood, and race is race,

And so, to mitigate disgrace,
He bought a most expensive beat
From Asprey's up to Oxford Street.

ANONYMOUS
In Katharine Whitehorn's *Only On Sundays*

Sire, four virgins wait without.
Without what?
Without food and clothing.
Give them food and bring them in.

W. H. AUDEN (1907–1973)
British poet
In *New Year Letter*, 1940

Men will pay large sums to whores
For telling them they are not bores.

BRIGITTE BARDOT (*b.* 1933)
French actress

Men are beasts, and even beasts don't behave as they do.

Said of her in *Time*, 20 November 1972

The most important sex symbol of all time.

SIMONE DE BEAUVOIR (*b.* 1908)
French writer
Quoted in *Esquire*

The division of the sexes is a biological fact, not an event in history.

MAX BEERBOHM (1872–1956)
British writer and caricaturist
In *The Pervasion of Rouge*

'After all,' as a pretty girl once said to me, 'women are a sex by themselves, so to speak.'

In *Zuleika Dobson*

Zuleika, on a desert island, would have spent most of her time in looking for a man's footprint.

TONIA BERG
British singer

Sex is like money – very nice to have but vulgar to talk about.

PAULINE BLACK
English rock singer (The Selecter)

As soon as I got to be 15 I became really, really miserable, and it carried on till I was 18 and left home and discovered drink and sex.

WILLIAM BLAKE (1757–1827)
British poet
In *Auguries of Innocence*

The harlot's cry from street to street
Shall weave old England's winding-sheet.

ANGIE BOWIE (*b.* 1953)
Fashion designer and model

I think Mick Jagger would be astounded and amazed if he realized to how many people he is not a sex symbol.

FANNY BRICE (1891–1951)
American comedienne

Men always fall for frigid women because they put on the best show.

BRIGID BROPHY (*b.* 1929)
Irish writer
On *Fanny Hill*

To my mind, the two most fascinating subjects in the universe are sex and the eighteenth century.

RITA MAE BROWN (*b.* 1944)
American writer

What's the point of being a lesbian if a woman is going to look and act like an imitation man?

Once you know what women are like, men get kind of boring. I'm not trying to put them down, I mean I like them sometimes as people, but sexually they're dull.

GEORGE BURNS (*b.* 1896)
American actor

There will always be a battle between the sexes because men and women want different things. Men want women and women want men.

KATE BUSH (*b.* 1958)
British singer

I think I'm going to have trouble because people tend to put the sexuality first. I hope they don't.

MIGUEL CERVANTES (1547–1616)
Spanish writer
In *Don Quixote*

Once a woman parts with her virtue, she loses the esteem even of the man whose vows and tears won her to abandon it.

DENISE COFFEY (*b.* 1936)
British actress
Quoted in *News of the World*

I am that twentieth-century failure, a happy under-sexed celibate.

MAUREEN COLQUHOUN
'Sayings of the Week' (*Observer*, 11 March 1979)

Prostitutes have a great therapeutic value.

JILLY COOPER (*b.* 1937)
British journalist

Sex is only the liquid centre of the great Newberry Fruit of friendship.

EDWARD DAHLBERG (*b.* 1900)
American writer
In *Reasons of the Heart* ('On Lust')

What most men desire is a virgin who is a whore.

MANDY RICE-DAVIES
Former British call-girl
On the Profumo affair, 1963

I am notorious. I will go down in history as another Lady Hamilton.

On being told that Lord Astor had denied that he had been to bed with her

Well, he would, wouldn't he?

BETTE DAVIS (*b.* 1908)
American actress
On Theda Bara

Miss Bara was Pestilence herself, her monumental wickedness would not have been tolerated by Caligula in his beatnik depths for one moment.

COLLEEN DEWHURST
Quoted in *New York Times*, 17 February 1974

We're living in a kind of pallid emotional time, we're so jaded we've almost managed to make sex boring; when somebody new approaches you, you're afraid you're being approached according to page 136.

DR CAROLINE DEYS
'Sayings of the Week' (*Observer*, 11 July 1976)

Just as most women like male gynaecologists, I think most men like lady vasectomists. One of my most masculine patients said: 'It's sort of natural taking off your trousers in front of a woman.'

MARLENE DIETRICH (*b.* 1901)
German actress

In America sex is an obsession, in other parts of the world it is a fact.

DIANA DORS (*b.* 1931)
British actress
Quoted in the *Observer*

Funny really. When you look at the things that go on these days, my story reads like Noddy.

JOHN DRYDEN (1631–1700)
British poet
In *Cymon and Iphigenia*

She hugg'd th' offender, and forgave th' offence, Sex to the last.

MARIANNE FAITHFULL (*b.* 1947)
British actress and rock singer

I wanted to be an actress and a scholar too. My first move was to get a Rolling Stone as a boyfriend. I slept with three then decided that the singer was the best bet.

EVA FIGES (*b.* 1932)
British writer
Quoted in *Reader's Digest*

When modern women discovered the orgasm it was, combined with modern birth control, perhaps the biggest single nail in the coffin of male dominance.

BETTY FORD
Wife of former US President

They've asked me everything but how often I sleep with my husband. And if they'd asked me that, I would have told them, 'As often as possible'.

MARILYN FRENCH (*b.* 1929)
American novelist

All men are rapists and that's all they are. They rape us with their eyes, their laws, and their codes.

BETTY FRIEDAN (*b.* 1921)
American feminist

Sex is the only frontier open to women who have always lived within the confines of the feminine mystique.

ZSA ZSA GABOR (*b.* 1919)
Hungarian-born actress

If they had as much adultery going on in New York as they said in the divorce courts, they . . . would never have a chance to make the beds at the Plaza.

JANE GALLION

You're used. Used by what you are, eat, believe and who you sleep with. You can stop it. If you want equality, it has to start in bed. If he won't give it to you there, rip him off.

JEAN GIRAUDOUX (1882–1944)
French writer
In *Amphitryon 38*

To win a woman in the first place one must please her, then undress her, and then somehow get her clothes back on her. Finally, so that she will allow you to leave her, you've got to annoy her.

BETTY GRABLE (1916–1973)
American actress and WWII pin-up

I'm strictly an enlisted man's girl.

MARTHA GRAHAM (*b.* 1894)
American dancer and choreographer

The body never lies.

GERMAINE GREER (*b.* 1939)
Australian feminist

The real theatre of the sex war is the domestic hearth.

Quoted in *The Times*, 3 February 1973

Despite a lifetime of service to the cause of sexual liberation, I have never caught venereal disease, which makes me feel rather like an Arctic explorer who has never had frostbite.

DEBBIE HARRY (*b.* 1941)
American rock singer

The concentration on my sexuality is the result of honesty. It's my own fault. By talking. By being real. If I was unreal it would be much easier. Unreal about what I was.

MOLLY HASKELL
Quoted in *Newsweek*, 21 June 1971

They have gone from Puritanism into promiscuity without passing through sensuality.

NATHANIEL HAWTHORN (1804–1864)
American novelist
In *Journals*, 16 March

A woman's chastity consists, like an onion, of a series of coats.

LADY HILLINGDON (1857–1940)
British aristocrat and writer

I am happy now that Charles calls on my bedchamber less frequently than of old. As it is I now endure but two calls a week and when I hear his steps outside my door I lie down on my bed, close my eyes, open my legs and think of England.

SHERE HITE
American writer and sexologist

Like most women, most of what I knew about sex came from men.

OLIVER WENDELL HOLMES, SR. (1809–1894)
American writer

A woman never forgets her sex. She would rather talk with a man than an angel any day.

MARSHA HUNT
American singer

I feel sexless on stage, I'm neither man nor woman. A lot of people think I'm terribly butch.

CLYDE JEAVONS & JEREMY PASCALL
In *A Pictorial History of Sex in the Movies*

By 1920 Bara's screen career was at an end. Her contribution to the art of the film was negligible, but her contribution to the making of the sex symbol . . . was considerable.

JILL JOHNSTON (*b.* 1920)
American feminist

Bisexuality is not so much a cop-out as a fearful compromise.

BIANCA JAGGER
Former wife of Mick Jagger
To Warren Beatty

So we had an affair. You must be pretty bad, I don't even remember you.

JOAN JETT
American punk rock singer

Girls got balls. They're just a little higher up, that's all.

ERICA JONG (*b.* 1942)
American writer
In *Fear of Flying*

Men and women, women and men. It will never work.

ERICH KÄSTNER (*b.* 1899)
German writer

Recently and in the middle of bed, a girl student of law informed me that virginity might possibly be quite nice, but had now hardly any collector's value.

CHRISTINE KEELER (*b.* 1942)
Former British call-girl

I'm on the gravy train with a second-class ticket.

JACQUELINE KENNEDY ONASSIS (*b.* 1929)
After the assassination of her husband

The American public would forgive me anything except running off with Eddie Fisher.

RUDYARD KIPLING (1865–1936)
British writer
In *The Ladies*

For the Colonel's Lady an' Judy O'Grady
Are sisters under their skins!

D. H. LAWRENCE (1855–1930)
British novelist and poet
In *Pornography and Obscenity*

If a woman hasn't got a tiny streak of a harlot in her, she's a dry stick as a rule.

HELEN LAWRENSON
American journalist

Whatever else can be said about sex, it cannot be called a dignified performance.

As for that topsy-turvy tangle known as *soixante-neuf*, personally I have always felt it to be madly confusing, like trying to pat your head and rub your stomach at the same time.

FRAN LEBOWITZ (*b. circa* 1951)
American journalist
In *Metropolitan Life*, 1978

Girls who put out are tramps. Girls who don't are ladies. This is, however, a rather archaic use of the word. Should one of you boys happen upon a girl who doesn't put out, do not jump to the conclusion that you have found a lady. What you have probably found is a lesbian.

GYPSY ROSE LEE (1914–1970)
American stripper

Men aren't attracted to me by my mind. They're attracted by what I don't mind.

I'm a bit of a prude myself.

Royalties are nice and all, but shaking the beads brings in money quicker.

OSCAR LEVANT (1906–1972)
American pianist
On Doris Day

I knew her before she was a virgin.

ANITA LOOS (*b.* 1893)
American novelist
Quoted in *New York Herald Tribune*, 1974

If we have to kiss Hollywood goodbye, it may be with one of those tender, old-fashioned, seven-second kisses as exchanged between two people of the opposite sex with all their clothes on.

SOPHIA LOREN (*b.* 1934)
Italian actress

Sex appeal is fifty per cent what you've got and fifty per cent what people think you've got.

'Sayings of the Week' (*Observer*)

If you play sexiness deliberately, the audience senses the phoniness.

LINDA LOVELACE
Former American porno star
Quoted in *Now!*, 1981

I would like to see all people who read pornography or have anything to do with it put in a mental hospital for observation so we could find out what we have done to them.

SUZANNE LOWRY
In *The Guardian*, 24 May 1974
On prostitution

Keeping body and soul together is never as difficult as trying to keep them separate.

LUCIA
A prostitute
In a speech to COYOTE Convention, June 1974

It's a gentleman's trip. A man propositions you, a man busts you, a man judges you, a man jails you, and a man bails you out.

JOANNA LUMLEY (*b.* 1946)
British actress

Sex symbol? I am non-toxic, safe. Girls write to me asking for photographs to send to their boyfriends.

LORETTA LYNN
American singer

I didn't know how babies were made until I was pregnant with my fourth child.

MARY MCCARTHY (*b.* 1912)
American writer

Europeans used to say Americans were puritanical. Then they discovered that we were not puritans. So now they say we are obsessed with sex.

MARSHALL MCLUHAN (1911–1980)
American social scientist
In *The Mechanical Bride*

To the mind of the modern girl, legs, like busts, are power points which she has been taught to tailor, but as parts of the success kit rather than erotically or sensuously.

BETTY MACDONALD (*d.* 1958)
American writer
In *The Egg and I*

I can feel for her because, although I have never been an Alaskan prostitute, dancing on the bar in a spangled dress, I still get very bored with washing and ironing and dishwashing and cooking day after relentless day.

SHIRLEY MACLAINE (*b.* 1934)
American actress

I've made so many movies playing a hooker that they don't pay me in the regular way any more. They leave it on the dresser.

MIGNON MCLAUGHLIN
American writer

Many are saved from sin by being so inept at it.

WILLIAM MANCHESTER (*b.* 1922)
American writer

Marilyn Monroe could make both ends meet by posing naked for girlie photographs, the most provocative of which was reproduced in vivid colour on the tip of a best-selling condom.

BETTE MIDLER (*b.* 1945)
American entertainer

I said to my boyfriend, Ernie, 'You gotta kiss me where it smells,' so he drove me to Wapping.

MAX MILLER (1895–1963)
British comedian
In *The Max Miller Blue Book*

Jack and Jill went up the hill
Just like two cock linnets,
Jill came down with half a crown –
She wasn't up there two minutes.

KATE MILLETT (*b.* 1934)
American feminist

Love is the only circumstance in which the female is (ideologically) pardoned for sexual activity.

There is no such thing as homosexual or heterosexual . . . We're so uptight about sensuality that the only people we can stroke as expressions of affection are children and dogs.

Prostitution is . . . the very core of the female's social condition . . . It is not sex the prostitute is really made to see: it is degradation.

MISTINGUETT (1874–1956)
French dancer

A kiss can be a comma, a question mark or an exclamation point. That's basic spelling that every woman ought to know.

MARILYN MONROE (1926–1962)
American actress
In Jeremy Pascall and Clyde Jeavons' *A Pictorial History of Sex in the Movies*

A sex symbol becomes a thing. I hate being a thing.

. . . I don't mind living in a man's world as long as I can be a woman in it.

MICHEL DE MONTAIGNE (1533–1592)
French essayist

The daughter-in-law of Pythagoras said that a woman who

goes to bed with a man ought to lay aside her modesty with her skirt, and put it on again with her petticoat.

MARABEL MORGAN

In *Variety is the Spice of Sex*.

Tonight, after the children are in bed, place a lighted candle on the floor and seduce him under the dining-room table.

LLOYD MORRIS

In *Not So Long Ago*

Miss Bara made voluptuousness a common American commodity, as accessible as chewing gum.

ALICE MUNRO

In *Something I've Been Meaning to Tell You*

I read a book called *The Art of Loving*. A lot of things seemed clear while I was reading it but afterwards I went back to being more or less the same.

EDNA O'BRIEN (*b.* 1936)

Irish writer

In D. Bailey's *Goodbye Baby and Amen*

Permissiveness is simply removing the dust sheets from our follies.

ARISTOTLE ONASSIS (1906–1975)

Greek shipping tycoon, second husband of Jacqueline Kennedy

Jackie is like a little bird that needs its freedom as well as its security, and she gets them both from me.

DOROTHY PARKER (1893–1967)

American writer and wit

That woman can speak eighteen languages and she can't say 'No' in any of them.

His voice was as intimate as the rustle of sheets.

DOLLY PARTON
American singer
On her breasts

If I hadn't had them, I would have had some made.

CYNTHIA PAYNE
English madam

It's my ambition to open a home for the elderly . . . If people wanted sex they could charge it to the National Health.

PRISCILLA PRESLEY
American widow of Elvis Presley
While lying on the beach between Elvis and Tom Jones

Boy wouldn't thirty million women like to be where I am now.

PUBLILIUS SYRUS (1st century BC)
In *Moral Sayings*

Venus yields to caresses, not to compulsion.

SUZI QUATRO (*b.* 1950)
American rock singer

I sure ain't no lady . . . playing the bass is so horny. It gets you right between the legs.

Being a sex symbol is the furthest thing from my mind.

DR RENEE RICHARDS
American doctor who changed sex

A transsexual loves women so much he wants to join them.

No one would undergo a sex change for a reason as shallow as playing tennis.

LINDA RONSTADT (*b.* 1946)
American rock singer
My big fantasy is to seduce a priest.

In all of the world outside of California, if you don't wear a bra, it supposedly means you want to fuck everybody. I don't.

I have to get sort of animal for what I do.

On learning the facts of life, aged 7.

My cousin Phil told me. He was a year older than I was. My mom was pregnant with my little brother and my cousin said, 'I know what your parents have been doing.' I said, 'No, my parents don't do that – they wouldn't.'

HELEN ROWLAND (1875–1956)
American journalist

No man can understand why a woman should prefer a good reputation to a good time.

A Bachelor of Arts is one who makes love to a lot of women and yet has the art to remain a bachelor.

A bachelor has to have inspiration for making love to a woman – a married man needs only an excuse.

CHARLOTTE Y. SALISBURY
Family planning slogan, India
In *Asian Diary*, 1968

Loop before you leap.

MARGARET SANGER (1833–1966)
Leader of American birth control movement

No woman can call herself free who does not own and control her body. No woman can call herself free until she can choose consciously whether she will or will not be a mother.

GRACE SLICK (*b.* 1939)
American rock singer
On paying a $2000 car repair bill and finding the car still wouldn't go

I don't mind getting screwed but at least I like to come.

PAGE SMITH & CHARLES DANIEL
In *The Chicken Book*

All animals are sad after making love except the rooster and the human female.

PATTI SMITH (*b.* 1946)
American rock singer

I used to dream of getting fucked by the Holy Ghost when I was a kid.

SUSAN SONTAG (*b.* 1933)
American writer

There are some elements of life, above all sexual pleasure, about which it isn't necessary to have a position.

The two pioneering forces of modern sensibility are Jewish moral seriousness and homosexual aestheticism and irony.

SPANISH PROVERB

The only chaste woman is the one who has not been asked.

MR JUSTICE STABLER
'Sayings of the Week' (*Observer*, 8 January 1961)

It would be much better if young women should stop being raped much earlier in the proceedings than some of them do.

SALLY STANFORD
American madam

No man can be held throughout the day by what happens throughout the night.

GLORIA STEINEM (*b.* 1934)
American feminist

A woman reading *Playboy* feels a little like a Jew reading a Nazi manual.

TOM STOPPARD (*b.* 1937)
British playwright

A lady, if surprised by melancholy, might go to bed with a chap, once; or a thousand times if consumed by passion. But twice, Wagner, *twice* . . . a lady might think she'd been taken for a tart.

VERA STRAVINSKY
Quoted in *New York Times*, 11 May 1969

I like Paris. They don't talk so much of money, but more of sex.

POLY STYRENE (Marion Elliot) (*b.* 1960)
British punk rock singer

Sex to me is a beautiful thing and shouldn't be abused. You shouldn't sleep with just anybody, you shouldn't sleep with anybody for money, you should sleep with somebody you really like and that's it. And it's not a power or control thing. That's what I don't like about sex. That's why I haven't slept with anyone for two years.

If somebody said I was a sex symbol I'd shave my head tomorrow.

TALLEYRAND (Charles Maurice de Talleyrand-Périgord) (1754–1838)
French statesman

Madame de Genlis, in order to avoid the scandal of coquetry, always yielded easily.

ELIZABETH TAYLOR (*b.* 1932)
British-born film star

Sex, treated properly, can be one of the most gorgeous things in the world.

TERENCE (190–159 BC)
Roman poet and playwright

I know the disposition of women: when you will, they

won't: when you won't, they set their hearts upon you of their own inclination.

CHERRY VANILLA (*b.* 1944)
American 'groupie' and actress

Never do with your hands what you could do better with your mouth.

Groupie? I was just a Superfan. Another girl looking for romance.

BARONESS VICKERS
British politician
'Sayings of the Week' (*Observer*)

Women would not be prostitutes if it were not for men.

RAQUEL WELCH (*b.* 1940)
American film star

I'm a late bloomer. My mind and my experience have caught up to my body.

Being a sex symbol was rather like being a convict.

TUESDAY WELD (*b.* 1943)
American actress

When grown-ups do it it's kind of dirty – that's because there's no one to punish them.

MAE WEST (1892–1980)
American film star

Sex is an emotion in motion.

MARY WHITEHOUSE (*b.* 1910)
Secretary, British Viewers' and Listeners' Association

Sex is important, but by no means the only important thing in life.

TOYAH WILLCOX (*b.* 1958)
British actress and rock singer

If I could turn the tables, I'd be a man. Or a hermaphrodite.

I think of myself as asexual . . . I don't like being a woman and I don't like being with other women. I don't like being bettered by a woman. It's my mother hatred coming out.

HARRIETTE WILSON (1789–1846)
Fashionable courtesan

My book has sold well but I get more for suppressing than for publishing and I will keep no one's name out for less than £200.

MARRIAGE

POLLY ADLER (1900–1962)
American madam

A house is not a home.

JOSEPH ADDISON (1672–1719)
British essayist

A woman seldom asks advice before she has bought her wedding clothes.

SHANA ALEXANDER
American broadcaster and journalist

When two people marry they become in the eyes of the law one person, and that one person is the husband.

ANONYMOUS WIFE
On retirement

Twice as much husband on half as much money.

ANONYMOUS DIVORCED WIFE OF PHYSICIAN
Quoted in *New York Times*

Doctors are difficult people to live with because nobody ever says no to them.

ANONYMOUS WOMAN
Quoted as epigraph to Erica Jong's *Fear of Flying*

Bigamy is having one husband too many. Monogamy is the same.

ANONYMOUS WOMAN
Quoted in the *Observer*'s survey on marriage, 1972

Marriage is the price I pay for having hormones.

ARISTOPHANES (446–380 BC)
Greek playwright
In *Lysistrata*

It's hard for women, you know,
To get away. There's so much to do.
Husbands to be patted and put in good tempers;
Servants to be poked out: children washed
Or soothed with lullays or fed with mouthfuls of pap.

ANTONY ARMSTRONG-JONES (Lord Snowdon)
(*b.* 1930)
British photographer, former husband of Princess Margaret

I have learned only two things are necessary to keep one's wife happy. First, let her think she is having her own way. Second, let her have it.

JANE AUSTEN (1775–1817)
British novelist
In *Pride and Prejudice*

Next to being married, a girl likes to be crossed in love a little now and then.

It is a truth universally acknowledged that a single man in possession of a good fortune must be in want of a wife.

A lady's imagination is very rapid: it jumps from admiration to love, from love to matrimony in a moment.

LAUREN BACALL (*b.* 1924)
American actress

Hollywood is the only place in the world where an amicable divorce means each one gets fifty per cent of the publicity.

FRANCIS BACON (1561–1626)
British philosopher
In *Essays* (On 'Marriage and Single Life')

He that hath wife and children hath given hostages to fortune; for they are impediments to great enterprises, either of virtue or mischief.

Wives are young men's mistresses; companions for middle age; and old men's nurses.

He was reputed one of the wise men that made answer to the question, when a man should marry? 'A young man not yet, an elder man not at all.'

In *The World*

What is it then to have or have no wife
But single thraldom, or a double strife?

WALTER BAGEHOT (1826–1877)
British economist and journalist

Women – one half the human race at least – care fifty times more for a marriage than a ministry.

LUCILLE BALL (*b.* 1910)
American actress

Divorce is defeat . . . It's an adult failure.

BRIGITTE BARDOT (*b.* 1933)
French actress

In marriage you are chained, it is an obligation; living with someone is a mutual agreement that is renegotiated and re-endorsed every day.

VICKI BAUM (1896–1960)
American writer

Marriage always demands the greatest understanding of the art of insincerity possible between two human beings.

ANNE BAXTER
American actress

I knew her when she didn't know where her next husband was coming from.

SIMONE DE BEAUVOIR (*b.* 1908)
French writer

The role of a retired person is no longer to possess one.

To catch a husband is an art; to hold him is a job.

Harmony between two individuals is never granted – it has to be conquered indefinitely.

Marriage is traditionally the destiny offered to women by society. Most women are married or have been, or plan to be or suffer from not being.

BIBLE
In *Proverbs* 18:22

Whoso findeth a wife findeth a good thing.

In *Proverbs* 21:9 and 25:24

It is better to dwell in a corner of the housetop, than with a brawling woman in a wide house.

AMBROSE BIERCE (1824–1914)
American writer
In *The Devil's Dictionary*

Bride, *n.* A woman with a fine prospect of happiness behind her.

WILLIAM BLAKE (1757–1827)
British poet

When a man has married a wife, he finds out whether Her knees and elbows are only glued together.

THE COUNTESS OF BLESSINGTON (Marguerite) (1789–1849)
Novelist

Love matches are made by people who are content, for a month of honey, to condemn themselves to a life of vinegar.

PAT BOONE (*b.* 1934)
American singer

When you get married you forget about kissing other women.

ELIZABETH BOWEN (1899–1973)
Anglo-Irish writer
In *The House in Paris*

That is partly why women marry – to keep up the fiction of being in the hub of things.

CHARLES BOYER (1897–1978)
French actor

A Frenchwoman, when double-crossed, will kill her rival; the Italian woman would rather kill her deceitful lover; the Englishwoman simply breaks off relations – but they all will console themselves with another man.

GYLES BRANDRETH (*b.* 1948)
British writer and broadcaster
In *The Complete Husband* ('Husband as Lover – Bedroom Manners')

Don't shriek loudly when your loved one puts a tender but chilly arm round you. Bear cold feet with fortitude.
Don't comment appreciatively on the charms of the leading lady on the late-night movie on television and then roll over, saying 'I'm tired'.
Don't grab all the bedclothes.
Don't ignore your wife's decision to put on her ultra-sexy black nightie, or her decision to sleep naked, when usually she dons several layers and bedsocks.

VERA BRITTAIN (1893–1970)
British novelist

I know one husband and wife who, whatever the official reasons given to the court for the break-up of their marriage, were really divorced because the husband believed that nobody ought to read while he was talking and the wife that nobody ought to talk while she was reading.

DR JOYCE BROTHERS (*b.* 1929)
American psychologist

For some reason, we see divorce as a signal of failure despite the fact that each of us has a right and an obligation to rectify any other mistake we make in life.

JIM BROWN (*b.* 1936)
American athlete and actor

In our society it is an advantage to a young lady to be married rather than to live with somebody. So, if you love a young lady, why not give her all of the advantages.

JEAN DE LA BRUYÈRE (1645–1696)
French writer
In *Characters*

There are few wives so perfect as not to give their husbands at least once a day good reason to repent of ever having married, or at least of envying those who are unmarried.

PEARL S. BUCK (1892–1973)
American novelist
In *To My Daughters, With Love* ('Man, Woman and Child')

If woman is to recapture the lost companionship with man and child, she must once more forget herself, as she did in the old pioneer days, and follow them into the world.

In *To My Daughters, With Love* ('Love and Marriage')

The bitterest creature under heaven is the wife who discovers that her husband's bravery is only bravado, that his strength is only a uniform, that his power is but a gun in the hands of a fool.

RICHARD BURTON (*b.* 1925)
British actor, former husband of Elizabeth Taylor

Elizabeth and I have been through too much to watch our marriage go up in flames. There is too much love going for us ever to divorce.

LORD BYRON (1788–1824)
British poet
In *To Eliza*

Though women are angels, yet wedlock's the devil.

MRS PATRICK CAMPBELL (1865–1940)
British actress

Marriage is the deep, deep peace of the double bed after the hurly-burly of the chaise-longue.

ALFRED CAPUS (1858–1922)
French writer
In *Notes et pensées*

To marry a woman you love and who loves you is to lay a wager with her as to who will stop loving the other first.

BARBARA CARTLAND (*b.* 1904)
British novelist
Quoted in *Daily Mail*

No young man ever suggested anything to me but a wedding ring. They were emotional, violent in their protestations of love, and three men swore they would kill themselves if I wouldn't marry them. But I was untouched, adored, worshipped and wooed.

HRH PRINCE CHARLES (*b.* 1948)

Falling madly in love with someone is not necessarily the starting point to getting married.

CHER (*b.* 1946)
American singer

The only grounds for divorce in California are marriage.

Being married to Greg Allman was like going to Disneyland on acid. You knew you had a good time but you just couldn't remember.

G. K. CHESTERTON (1874–1936)
British essayist and novelist

Variability is one of the virtues of a woman. It avoids the crude requirement of polygamy. So long as you have one good wife you are sure to have a spiritual harem.

WINSTON S. CHURCHILL (1874–1965)
British statesman
In *My Early Life: A Roving Commission*

Events were soon to arise in the fiscal sphere which were to plunge me into new struggles and absorb my thoughts and energies at least until September 1908, when I married and lived happily ever afterwards.

COLETTE (Sidonie-Gabrielle) (1873–1954)
French writer
In *Earthly Paradise* ('Wedding Day')

There is no need to waste pity on young girls who are having their moments of disillusionment, for in another moment they will recover their illusion.

Girls usually have a papier-mâché face on their wedding day.

In *The Wit of Women*

The only really masterful noise a man ever makes in a house is the noise of his key, when he is still on the landing, fumbling for the lock.

HELOISE CRUSE
Quoted in *Saturday Evening Post*, 2 March 1963

The graveyards are full of women whose houses were so spotless you could eat off the floor. Remember the second wife always has a maid.

EVELYN CUNNINGHAM
In a speech at Women's Symposium, New York, 16 May 1969

Women are the only oppressed group in our society that lives in intimate association with our oppressors.

RODNEY DANGERFIELD (*b.* 1921)
American actor

We sleep in separate rooms, we have dinner apart, we take separate vacations – we're doing everything we can to keep our marriage together.

FLORA DAVIS

Almost all married people fight, although many are ashamed to admit it. Actually a marriage in which no quarrelling at all takes place may well be one that is dead or dying from emotional undernourishment. If you care, you probably fight.

ELEANOR DIENSTAG
Quoted in *Psychology Today*, March 1977

Moving from marriage to divorce is like travelling to a foreign country. Few of us are eager for the journey; few can afford the fare; and few know how to cope en route or what to expect when we arrive.

BRITT EKLAND (*b.* 1943)
Swedish actress, renowned for her many liaisons

I know a lot of people didn't expect our relationship to last – but we've just celebrated our two months' anniversary.

GEORGE ELIOT (Marian Evans) (1819–1880)
British novelist

I should like to know what is the proper function of women if it is not to make reasons for husbands to stay at home, and still stronger reasons for bachelors to go out.

In *Middlemarch*

Having once embarked on your marital voyage, it is impossible not to be aware that you make no way and that the sea is not within sight – that, in fact, you are exploring an enclosed basin.

RALPH WALDO EMERSON (1803–1882)
In *Journals*

A man's wife has more power over him than the state has.

EURIPIDES (484–406 BC)
Greek playwright
In *Andromache*

What else goes wrong for a woman – except her marriage?

All other woes a woman bears are minor
But lose her husband! – might as well be dead.

A woman, even when married to a cad,
Ought to be deferential, not a squabbler.

HENRY FIELDING (1707–1754)
British novelist

When widows exclaim loudly against second marriage, I would always lay a wager that the man, if not the wedding day, is absolutely fixed on.

ZELDA FITZGERALD (1900–1948)
Wife of Scott Fitzgerald
Quoted in *New York Times*, 13 August 1967

It is the loose ends with which men hang themselves.

JANE FONDA (*b.* 1937)
American actress

God, for two people to be able to live together for the rest of their lives is almost unnatural.

BENJAMIN FRANKLIN (1706–1790)
American statesman
In *Poor Richard's Almanack*

You can bear your own faults, and why not a fault in your wife?

THOMAS FULLER (1608–1661)
British writer
In *Gnomologia*

A man's best fortune, or his worst, is his wife.

In *Holy and Profane State*

He knows little who will tell his wife all he knows.

ZSA ZSA GABOR (*b.* 1919)
Hungarian-born actress

Getting divorced just because you don't love a man is almost as silly as getting married just because you do.

You never really know a man until you have divorced him.

Husbands are like fires – they go out when unattended.

I am a marvellous housekeeper. Every time I leave a man, I keep his house.

FRANCES DANA GAGE (1808–1884)
In *The Housekeeper's Soliloquy*

Wife, mother, nurse, seamstress, cook, housekeeper, chambermaid, laundress, dairy-woman, and scrub generally, doing the work of six, for the sake of being supported.

GRETA GARBO (*b.* 1905)
Swedish film star

I cannot see myself as a wife – ugly word.

MARY GARDEN (1874–1967)
American opera singer

Women marry because they don't want to work.

JOHN GAY (1685–1732)
British poet
In *The Beggar's Opera*

The comfortable estate of widowhood is the only hope that keeps up a wife's spirits.

JEAN GIRAUDOUX (1882–1944)
French writer
In *Amphitryon 38*

A wife loves out of duty, and duty leads to constraint, and constraint kills desire.

MAXIM GORKY (1868–1936)
Russian writer
In *The Lower Depths*

When a woman gets married it's like jumping into a hole in the ice in the middle of winter: you do it once, and you remember it the rest of your days.

GERMAINE GREER (*b.* 1939)
Australian feminist
In *The Female Eunuch*

Mother is the dead heart of the family, spending father's earnings on consumer goods to enhance the environment in which he eats, sleeps and watches television.

By the act of marriage you endorse all the ancient and dead values. You endorse things like monogamy. Lifelong monogamy is a maniacal idea.

KITTY HANSON
American writer
In *For Richer, For Poorer*

Next to the American corpse, the American bride is the hottest thing in today's merchandising market.

LADY HASLUCK
Wife of former Australian Governor-General

The worst thing about work in the house or home is that whatever you do it is destroyed, laid waste or eaten within twenty-four hours.

KATHARINE HEPBURN (*b.* 1909)
American actress

Sometimes I wonder if men and women really suit each other. Perhaps they should live next door and just visit now and then.

MRS HOFLAND
In *Fragments on Women*

How can a woman promise to honour and obey him whom

she feels to be her inferior? How can she condemn herself to daily, hourly intercourse with one, who can neither increase her knowledge, foster her virtues, nor even comprehend the capabilities she may possess, as a friend or a companion?

OLIVER WENDELL HOLMES, SR. (1809–1894)
American writer
In *The Professor at the Breakfast Table*

I should like to see any kind of a man, distinguishable from a gorilla, that some good and even pretty woman could not shape a husband out of.

EDGAR WATSON HOWE (1853–1937)
British writer
In *Country Town Sayings*

At first a woman doesn't want anything but a husband, but just as soon as she gets one, she wants everything else in the world.

VIRGINIA CARY HUDSON
In *O Ye Jigs and Juleps*, 1962

I guess walking slow getting married is because it gives you time to maybe change your mind.

WASHINGTON IRVING (1783–1859)
On 'The Wife'

No man knows what the wife of his bosom is until he has gone with her through the fiery trials of this world.

HENRY JAMES (1843–1916)
American writer
In *The Golden Bowl*

She would have liked for instance . . . to marry; and nothing in general is more ridiculous, even when it has been pathetic, than a woman who has tried and has not been able.

DR SAMUEL JOHNSON (1709–1784)
British writer
In *Boswell's Life of Dr Johnson*

He that outlives a wife whom he has long loved, sees himself disjoined from the only mind that has the same hopes, and fears, and interest; from the only companion with whom he has shared much good and evil; and with whom he could set his mind at liberty, to retrace the past or anticipate the future.

PENELOPE KEITH
British actress

All women should marry younger men. After all, men reach their sexual prime at 19 and women can reach it at 90.

ROSE KENNEDY (*b.* 1890)
Mother of President John F. Kennedy

I've had an exciting life. I married for love and got a little money along with it.

JEAN KERR (*b.* 1923)
American writer

Marrying a man is like buying something you've been admiring for a long time in a shop window. You may love it when you get home, but it doesn't always go with everything else in the house.

BILLIE JEAN KING (*b.* 1943)
American tennis player

Marriage isn't a 50–50 proposition very often. It's more like 100-0 one moment and 0–100 the next.

ANN LANDERS (*b.* 1918)
American journalist

Sensual pleasures have the fleeting brilliance of a comet; a happy marriage has the tranquillity of a lovely sunset.

A successful marriage is not a gift; it is an achievement.

EMMA LEE

Not all women give most of their waking thoughts to the problem of pleasing men. Some are married.

GEORGE, LORD LYTTELTON (1709–1773)
In *An Irregular Ode*

How much the wife is dearer than the bride.

WILLIAM MCFEE (1881–1966)
British writer
In *Knights and Turcopoliers*

The wives who are not deserted, but who have to feed and clothe and comfort and scold and advise, are the true objects of commiseration; wives whose existence is given over to a ceaseless vigil of cantankerous affection.

PHYLLIS McGINLEY (*b.* 1905)
Canadian writer
On 'How to Get Along with Men'

Marriage was all a woman's idea, and for man's acceptance of the pretty yoke it becomes us to be grateful.

DEAN MARTIN (*b.* 1917)
American film actor and singer

In Hollywood if a guy's wife looks like a new woman – she probably is.

MARGARET MEAD (1901–1978)
American anthropologist

Having two bathrooms ruined the capacity to cooperate.

The wife in curlpapers is replaced by the wife who puts on lipstick before she wakens her husband.

NAOMI MITCHISON (*b.* 1897)
British writer
Quoted in *The Times*, 1979

Being married is a value: it is bread and butter, but it may make one less able to provide the cake.

NANCY MITFORD (1904–1973)
British writer
In *The Pursuit of Love*

The high spirits, which . . . he had seemed to possess, must have been due to youth, drink and good health. Now that he was grown up and married he put all three resolutely behind him.

HENRI DE MONTHERLANT (1896–1972)
French novelist and playwright
In *Young Girls*

The man who marries always makes the woman a present because she needs marriage and he does not . . . Woman is made for man, man is made for life.

MARIANNE MOORE (1887–1972)
American poet
In *Marriage*

Psychology which explains everything
explains nothing,
and we are still in doubt.

MARILYN MONROE (1926–1962)
American actress

Husbands are chiefly good lovers when they are betraying their wives.

MARABEL MORGAN

Love in marriage is commitment. Commitment involves a woman's full surrender to her man.

FRANK MUIR (*b.* 1919) & DENIS NORDEN (*b.* 1922)
British humorists

It has been said that a bride's attitude towards her betrothed can be summed up in three words: Aisle, Altar, Hymn.

IRIS MURDOCH (*b.* 1919)
British philosopher and novelist
In *A Severed Head*

In almost every marriage there is a selfish and an unselfish partner. A pattern is set up and soon becomes inflexible, of one person always making the demands and one person always giving way.

'We aren't getting anywhere. You know that as well as I do.'
'One doesn't have to get anywhere in a marriage. It's not a public conveyance.'

LUCI JOHNSON NUGENT
Daughter of former President Lyndon Johnson

Every bride has to learn it's not her wedding but her mother's.

S. J. PERELMAN (1904–1970)
American writer

Do young men nowadays still become hopelessly enamoured of married women easily ten years their senior who have mocking, humorous mouths, eyes filled with tender raillery, and indulgent husbands? Back in the twenties, when it was a lot easier for a woman to be ten years my senior than it is now, I was privileged to know one who fitted these specifications.

KATHRIN PERUTZ
In *Marriage Is Hell*, 1972

Marriage is the hell of false expectations, where both partners, expecting to be loved, defined and supported, abdicate responsibility for themselves and accuse the other of taking away freedom.

ELIZABETH POST
Journalist

For some reason, it seems that the bride generally has to make more effort to achieve a successful marriage than the bridegroom.

DON RICKLES
American writer

Eddie Fisher married to Elizabeth Taylor is like me trying to wash the Empire State Building with a bar of soap.

HELEN ROWLAND (1875–1950)
American journalist

When a girl marries, she exchanges the attentions of many men for the inattention of one.

A husband is what is left of a man after the nerve is extracted.

When you see what some girls marry, you realize how they must hate to work for a living.

Never trust a husband too far, nor a bachelor too near.

It isn't tying himself to one woman that a man dreads when he thinks of marrying; it's separating himself from all the others.

Before marriage a man will lie awake all night thinking about something you said; after marriage he will fall asleep before you have finished saying it.

One man's folly is another man's wife.

In olden times sacrifices were made at the altar – a practice which is still continued.

Love, the quest; marriage, the conquest; divorce, the inquest.

BERTRAND RUSSELL (1872–1970)
British philosopher
In *Marriage and Morals* ('Prostitution')

Marriage is for women the commonest mode of livelihood, and the total amount of undesired sex endured by women is probably greater in marriage than in prostitution.

ADELA ROGERS ST JOHN (*b.* 1894)
American writer
Quoted in *Los Angeles Times*, 1974

I think every woman is entitled to a middle husband she can forget.

PHYLLIS SCHLAFLY (*b.* 1924)

Marriage is like panty-hose. It depends on what you put into it.

ANNE SEXTON
In *Housewife*

Some women marry houses,
It's another kind of skin, it has a heart,
a mouth, a liver and bowel movements.

GAIL SHEEHY (*b.* 1937)
American feminist

Marriage is a half step, a way to leave home without losing home.

SIMONE SIGNORET (*b.* 1921)
French actress
Quoted in *Daily Mail*, 4 July 1978

Chains do not hold a marriage together. It is threads, hundreds of tiny threads which sew people together through the years. That is what makes a marriage last – more than passion or even sex!

STEVIE SMITH (1902–1971)
British poet

There you are you see, quite simple, if you cannot have your dear husband for a comfort and a delight, for a breadwinner and a crosspatch, for a sofa, chair or a hot-water bottle, one can use him as a cross to be borne.

SUSAN SONTAG (*b.* 1933)
American essayist

You know I think rock 'n' roll is the reason I got divorced. I think it was Bill Haley and the Comets and Chuck Berry that made me decide that I had to get a divorce and leave the academic world.

GLORIA STEINEM (*b.* 1934)
American feminist

Jacqueline Onassis has a very clear understanding of marriage. I have a lot of respect for women who win the game with rules given you by the enemy.

Marriage makes you legally half a person, and what man wants to live with half a person?

ROSE PASTOR STOKES (1879–1933)
In *My Prayer*

Some pray to marry the man they love,
My prayer will somewhat vary:
I humbly pray to Heaven above
That I love the man I marry.

LADY SUMMERSKILL (1901–1980)
British politician

The so-called 'divorce reformer' can equally be called a marriage breaker.

BOOTH TARKINGTON (1869–1846)
American novelist
In *Looking Forward to the Great Adventure*

An ideal wife is any woman who has an ideal husband.

ELIZABETH TAYLOR (*b.* 1932)
British-born actress

I've only slept with the men I've been married to. How many women can make that claim?

MARGARET TRUDEAU (*b.* 1948)
Former wife of Canadian Prime Minister

It takes two to destroy a marriage.

ROBYN WALLIS
Documentary film-maker

I want to make people think about their relationships. I think it's very difficult to be happy, and very difficult, when you are married, to sustain a romantic relationship with your wife or husband.

JULIA MONTGOMERY WALSH
1 January 1967

If the value of a wife's services in a home were included in the US gross national income, that figure would double in a year.

CHARLES DUDLEY WARNER (1829–1900)
In *Third Story*

There isn't a wife in the world who has not taken the exact measure of her husband, weighed him and settled him in her own mind, and knows him as well as if she had ordered him after designs and specifications of her own.

DEE WELLS
British journalist
Quoted in *Daily Herald*, 13 February 1964

Maybe show-business people don't share our twenty-years-of-mortgage, twenty-years-of-children, and have-you-put-the-cat-out view of marriage.

MAE WEST (1892–1980)
American film star

Marriage is a great institution, but I'm not ready for an institution yet.

KATHARINE WHITEHORN & AURIOL STEVENS
British Journalists
In the *Observer*

. . . if a Lady Chesterfield were writing to a daughter today she might well advise her, should she want a life of unmixed domesticity, to take care to become a second wife, not a first. By the time a man's on to his second, she might suggest, he may well have reached an age when a bit of peaceful slipper-warming is welcome; but if you're a first-time-around wife – watch out.

OSCAR WILDE (1854–1900)
Irish writer
In *The Importance of Being Earnest*

The amount of women in London who flirt with their own husbands is perfectly scandalous. It looks so bad. It is simply washing one's clean linen in public.

THORNTON WILDER (*b.* 1898)
American writer
In *The Matchmaker*

Marriage is a bribe to make a housekeeper think she's a householder.

SHELLEY WINTERS (*b.* 1922)
American actress

In Hollywood all marriages are happy. It's trying to live together afterward that causes problems.

CHILDREN

SHANA ALEXANDER
American journalist and broadcaster

The ideal of American parenthood is to be a kid with your kid.

PRINCESS ANNE (*b.* 1950)

Being pregnant is a very boring six months. I am not particularly maternal. It's an occupational hazard of being a wife.

CONSUELO S. BAEHR
In *Report from the Heart*

I am on trial every time they (the children) sit down to eat, every time they put on a white shirt.

BERYL BAINBRIDGE (*b.* 1934)
British writer
In *Injury Time*

Being constantly with children was like wearing a pair of shoes that were expensive and too small. She couldn't bear to throw them out, but they gave her blisters.

HONEY BANE (*b.* 1964)
British singer

I always used to be a bit weird. I went to school with knickers over me head when I was ten and I had red and green streaks in my hair.

HENRY WARD BEECHER (1813–1887)
American preacher

What the mother sings to the cradle goes all the way down to the coffin.

There is no slave out of heaven like a loving woman; and, of all loving women, there is no such slave as a mother.

ELISABETH BERESFORD
British children's writer
In *The Wombles*

Make Good Use of Bad Rubbish.

DEBBY BOONE
On her father, American Singer Pat Boone

I wish to thank my father for my strait-laced wholesome all-American image. It's like a big protective shield that keeps away all the smut and ugly things in life.

I was a teenage coffee addict. When I was younger, I always wanted it because adults were drinking it. But my dad, until I was fifteen, never let me drink it. Once I started, I wanted it always . . . it was such a great high. I didn't think it was real bad until I started getting shaky and having stomach aches. Sometimes I couldn't write my name on a cheque because my hands were shaking so much. Finally I had to go cold turkey.

MRS JANICE BRADSHAW
Quoted by Sargent Shriver, 12 April 1965

Poverty is taking your children to the hospital and spending the whole day waiting with no one even taking your name – and then coming back the next day, and the next, until they finally get around to you.

ELIZABETH BARRETT BROWNING (1806–1861)
British poet
In *The Cry of the Children*

Do ye hear the children weeping, O my brothers,
  Ere the sorrow comes with years?

PEARL S. BUCK (1892–1973)
American novelist
In *To My Daughters, With Love* ('To You on Your First Birthday')

Some are kissing mothers and some are scolding mothers, but it is love just the same, and most mothers kiss and scold together.

In *To My Daughters, With Love* ('What America Means to Me')

It is ironical that in an age when we have prided ourselves on our progress in the intelligent care and teaching of children we have at the same time put them at the mercy of new and most terrible weapons of destruction.

GELETT BURGESS (1866–1951)
American writer
In *The Maxims of Methuselah*

In the mind of a woman, to give birth to a child is the short cut to omniscience.

ELIAS CANETTI (*b.* 1905)
Bulgarian writer
In *Auto da Fé*

If a mother could be content to be nothing but a mother; but where would you find one who would be satisfied with that part alone?

MRS LILLIAN CARTER (*d.* 1983)
Mother of former US President Jimmy Carter

How could Jimmy ever criticize me? I'm his mama.

I love all my children, but some of them I don't like.

Jimmy says he'll never tell a lie. Well, I lie all the time. I have to – to balance the family ticket.

PHILA HENRIETTA CASE (fl. 1864)
In *Nobody's Child*

Oh! why does the wind blow upon me so wild?
Is it because I'm nobody's child?

HELEN CASTLE

Give the neighbour's kids an inch and they'll take a yard.

PHYLLIS CHESLER

In *About Men*, 1978

How sad that men would base an entire civilization on the principle of paternity, upon the legal ownership and presumed responsibility for children, and then never really get to know their sons and daughters very well.

If it were natural for fathers to care for their sons, they would not need so many laws commanding them to do so.

WINSTON S. CHURCHILL (1875–1965)

British statesman

On his mother, Jennie Jerome Churchill

In my interest she left no wire unpulled, no stone unturned, no cutlet uncooked.

COLETTE (Sidonie-Gabrielle) (1873–1954)

French writer

In Leta W. Clark's *Women, Women, Women*

You will do foolish things, but do them with enthusiasm.

JOAN COLLINS (*b.* 1933)

British-born actress

The easiest way to convince my kids that they don't really need something is to get it for them.

MARCELENE COX

American writer

Quoted in *Ladies Home Journal*, 1948

The illusions of childhood are necessary experiences. A child should not be denied a balloon because an adult knows that sooner or later it will burst.

RICHMAL CROMPTON (1890–1969)
British writer
In *Just William*

Violet Elizabeth dried her tears. She saw that they were useless and she did not believe in wasting her effects. 'All right,' she said calmly, 'I'll thcream then, I'll thcream, an' thcream, an' thcream till I'm thick.'

DANISH PROVERB

Who takes the child by the hand, takes the mother by the heart.

MARGARET DRABBLE (*b.* 1939)
British novelist
In *The Millstone*

Lord knows what incommunicable small terrors infants go through, unknown to all. We disregard them, we say they forget because they have not the words to make us remember . . . By the time they learn to speak they have forgotten the details of their complaints, and so we never know. They forget so quickly, we say, because we cannot contemplate the fact that they never forget.

RUTH DRAPER (1889–1956)
American variety artist
On 'The Children's Party'

Sometimes I think I'll not send him to school – but just let his individuality develop.

ISADORA DUNCAN (1878–1927)
American dancer

So long as little children are allowed to suffer, there is no true love in this world.

MRS EISENHOWER
Quoted in Doris Faber's *The Presidents' Mothers*, 1978
On being asked if she was proud of her son

Which one?

PAUL EHRLICH (1854–1915)
German bacteriologist

The mother of the year should be a sterilized woman with two adopted children.

RALPH WALDO EMERSON (1803–1882)
In *Journals*

There never was a child so lovely but his mother was glad to get him asleep.

IMOGENE FEY

A man finds out what is meant by a spitting image when he tries to feed cereal to his infant.

ELLEN FOLEY (*b.* 1950)
American rock singer

When I was a kid I put a lot of my energy into things like shoplifting. I got in a lot of trouble. I used to bite people.

ANNA FREUD (*b.* 1895)
Austrian-English psychoanalyst and daughter of Sigmund Freud

All the advantages of a later life may be wasted on a child who has lacked a warm and satisfying mother relationship.

PRINCESS GRACE OF MONACO (1928–1982)

With animals you don't see the male caring for the offspring. It's against nature. It is a woman's prerogative and duty, and a privilege.

KATHARINE HEPBURN (*b.* 1909)
American actress

Young people are digging a hole they'll never get out of.

JANE HOWARD

Boys will be boys these days and so, apparently, will girls.

SYDNEY J. HARRIS (*b.* 1917)
American journalist

The commonest fallacy among women is that simply having children makes one a mother – which is as absurd as believing that having a piano makes one a musician.

GEORGIA HOUSER
Quoted in *Newsweek*, 15 May 1978

We're the ultimate nuclear family, and sometimes I feel as if someone is trying to split the atom.

VICTOR HUGO (1802–1885)
French poet
In *Les Misérables*

A little girl without a doll is almost as unfortunate and quite as impossible as a woman without children.

FANNY HURST (1889–1968)
American novelist
Obituary in *New York Times*, 24 February 1968 (on wishing her mother had named her Beulah)

No one ever sat on her Beulah.

MARGARET JONES
On her son, rock singer David Bowie

He changes so, doesn't he? He's changing his views about everything all the time. He's like a chameleon. There'll never be a dictatorship here and why he says he wants one, I don't know.

SALLY KEMPTON (*b.* 1943)
American journalist

All children are potential victims, dependent on the world's goodwill.

JACQUELINE KENNEDY ONASSIS (*b.* 1929)
Wife of 35th President of the United States

If you bungle raising your children, I don't think whatever else you do well matters very much.

FLORYNCE KENNEDY (*b.* 1916)
American feminist
Quoted in *Ms*

Being a mother is a noble status, right? Right. So why does it change when you put 'unwed' or 'welfare' in front of it?

ROSE KENNEDY (*b.* 1890)
Mother of John F. Kennedy
Quoted by one of her twenty-nine grand-children in *Look*, 5 March 1979

She's a good lady. I don't think she knows all our names. She calls us all 'Dear'.

MARY LAMB (1764–1847)
British poet
In *Parental Recollections*

Thou, straggler into loving arms,
Young climber up of knees,
When I forget thy thousand ways,
Then life and all shall cease.

FELICIA LAMPORT
In *Scrap Irony*

The after-effects of a mother's neglects
May spoil her boy's orientation to sex,
But the converse is worse; if she over-protects,
The pattern of Oedipus wrecks.

JULIA LANG
British broadcaster
In *Listen With Mother*

Are you sitting comfortably? Then I'll begin.

FRAN LEBOWITZ (*c.* 1951)
American journalist
In *Metropolitan Life*

All God's children are not beautiful. Most of God's children are, in fact, barely presentable.

I am not personally a parent. But I do have two godchildren and am expecting a third. I am naturally concerned for their future. If I ruled the world you could bet your boots that none of them would ever set their eyes on any such contraptions as digital clocks and pocket calculators. But alas, I do not rule the world and that, I am afraid, is the story of my life – always a godmother, never a God.

RUBY MANIKAN
Indian church leader
'Sayings of the Week' (*Observer*, 30 March 1947)

If you educate a man you educate a person, but if you educate a woman you educate a family.

MARY MARSH

The only time a woman wishes she were a year older is when she is expecting a baby.

FLORIDA SCOTT-MAXWELL
American psychologist

No matter how old a mother is, she watches her middle-aged children for signs of improvement.

MARY MCCARTHY (*b.* 1912)
American writer

The only form of action open to a child is to break something or strike someone, its mother or another child; it cannot cause things to happen in the world.

LINDA McCARTNEY
Photographer
On her husband, Paul McCartney

At bedtime a stern word from their father is enough to send them running for help to their nurse.

SHIRLEY MACLAINE (*b.* 1934)
American actress

We had to analyse the whole of the motivation behind this insane need to propagate.

PHYLLIS MCGINLEY (*b.* 1905)
Canadian writer
In *The Province of the Heart* ('The Honour of Being a Woman')

Our bodies are shaped to bear children, and our lives are a working out of the processes of creation. All our ambitions and intelligence are beside that great elemental point.

MIGNON MCLAUGHLIN
American writer

Most of us become parents long before we have stopped being children.

The young are generally full of revolt, and are often pretty revolting about it.

MARGARET MEAD (1901–1978)
American anthropologist

We must have . . . a place where children can have a whole group of adults they can trust.

No matter how many communes anybody invents, the family always creeps back.

H. L. MENCKEN (1880–1956)
American critic
In *Notebooks*

It is now quite lawful for a Catholic woman to avoid

pregnancy by a resort to mathematics, though she is still forbidden to resort to physics and chemistry.

LIZA MINNELLI (*b.* 1946)
American singer and actress

It was no great tragedy being Judy Garland's daughter. I had tremendously interesting childhood years – except they had little to do with being a child.

JESSICA MITFORD (*b.* 1917)
British writer
In *Hons and Rebels*

Knowing few children of my own age, I envied the children of literature to whom interesting things were always happening; Oliver Twist was so *lucky* to live in a fascinating orphanage!

NANCY MITFORD (1904–1973)
British writer

I love children. Especially when they cry – for then someone takes them away.

C. E. MONTAGUE (1867–1928)
British writer
In *Dramatic Values*

A gifted small girl has explained that pins are a great means of saving life, 'by not swallowing them'.

MARIA MONTESSORI (1870–1952)
Italian educator

The first idea that the child must acquire, in order to be actively disciplined is that of the difference between good and evil; and the task of the educator lies in seeing that the child does not confound good with immobility, and evil with activity.

ANONYMOUS NANNY
In Jonathan Gathorne-Hardy's *The Unnatural History of the Nanny*, 1973

There are three sorts of sin: little sins, bigger ones, and taking off your shoes without undoing the laces.

ANONYMOUS NEGRO MOTHER
Quoted in *The Independent*, 18 September 1902

A young white boy's badness is simply the overflowing of young animal spirits; the black boy's badness is badness, pure and simple.

NANETTE NEWMAN
British actress
In *God Bless Love*

'I feel very sad for children left alone in war and I would like to love them but they never put their names in the paper.' (Liz, aged seven)

'It's a pity you have to fall in love with boys because they always pinch you.' (Beryl, aged seven)

FRIEDRICH WILHELM NIETZSCHE (1844–1900)
German philosopher
In *Thus Spoke Zarathustra*

Man is for woman a means: the end is always the child.

HANNAH NIXON
In Liz Smith's *The Mother Book*, 1978

On her son, Richard Nixon, former U.S. President
The best potato masher one could wish for.

DOROTHY LAW NOLTE

If a child lives with approval, he learns to live with himself.

MARY NORTON (*b.* 1903)
British children's writer
In *The Borrowers*

We don't talk fancy grammar and eat anchovy toast. But to live under the kitchen doesn't say we aren't educated.

DOROTHY PARKER (1893–1967)
American writer and wit

The best way to keep children home is to make the home atmosphere happy – and let the air out of the tyres.

GLORIA PITZER
1 January 1978

There's one advantage to the music the younger generation goes for today, nobody can whistle it.

SUZI QUATRO (*b.* 1950)
American rock singer

When I was a kid, really small, I saw my brother go to the bathroom . . . I tried to do it too . . . I stood over the toilet and tried to do it the same way. My mother came in and tried to explain. I was outraged and demanded to know if he could why couldn't I? I'm 23 and I still haven't changed. I want to know why I can't do it all.

AGNES REPPLIER (1858–1950)
American essayist

Too much rigidity on the part of teachers should be followed by a brisk spirit of insubordination on the part of the taught.

REBECCA RICHARDS

Oh, to be only half as wonderful as my child thought I was when he was small, and only half as stupid as my teenager now thinks I am.

BETTY ROLLIN
American feminist

The notion that the maternal wish and the activity of mothering are instinctive or biologically predestined is baloney.

ELEANOR ROOSEVELT (1884–1962)
Wife of 32nd President of the United States
Quoted in *Today's Health*, 2 October 1966

I think, at a child's birth, if a mother could ask a fairy godmother to endow it with the most useful gift, that gift would be curiosity.

ALICE ROSSI (*b*. 1922)
American feminist

Sons forget what grandsons wish to remember.

CARL SANDBURG (1878–1967)
American poet
Quoted in *The People, Yes*, 1936

Small girl: Sometime they'll give a war and nobody will come.

DR MILTON R. SAPIRSTEIN
In *Paradoxes of Everyday Life*, 1953

It is impossible for any woman to love her children twenty-four hours a day.

DOROTHY L. SAYERS (1883–1957)
British author
In *Clouds of Witness*

In my day we called that (behaviour) hysterics, and naughtiness, and we knew exactly how to deal with it.

PHYLLIS SCHLAFFY (*b*. 1924)

Most women would rather cuddle a baby than a typewriter or a machine.

SEVENTEEN-YEAR-OLD EGYPTIAN GIRL
In a papyrus letter *c.* 2000 BC, at the Metropolitan Museum of Art

Dear Mother: I'm all right. Stop worrying about me.

GEORGE BERNARD SHAW (1856–1950)
Irish playwright
In *Getting Married*

The one point on which all women are in furious secret rebellion against the existing law is the saddling of the right to a child with the obligation to become the servant of a man.

GAIL SHEEHY (*b.* 1937)

Although today there are many trial marriages . . . there is no such thing as a trial child.

RICHARD BRINSLEY SHERIDAN (1751–1816)
British playwright
In *St Patrick's Day*

A fluent tongue is the only thing a mother don't like her daughter to resemble her in.

CHINA SLICK
Daughter of Grace Slick

I like my name, but I want to change it to Susie.

GRACE SLICK (*b.* 1939)
American rock singer
On her pregnancy

Some people like to have animals around. I like animals but I thought I'd try a human being because they have more happening.

SOPHOCLES (496–406 BC)
Greek playwright
In *Phaedra*

Children are the anchors that hold a mother to life.

MURIEL SPARK (*b.* 1918)
British novelist
In *The Comforters*

Parents learn a lot from their children about coping with life.

NANCY DENNIS SPROAT (1766–1826)
In *Lullabies for Children*

How pleasant is Saturday night,
  When I've tried all the week to be good,
And not spoke a word that was bad,
  And obliged every one that I could.

GLORIA STEINEM (*b.* 1934)
American feminist

By the year 2000 we will, I hope, raise our children to believe in human potential, not God.

ANN TAYLOR (1782–1866)

One ugly trick has often spoiled
  The sweetest and the best;
Matilda, though a pleasant child,
  One ugly trick possessed,
Which, like a cloud before the skies,
Hid all her better qualities.

JANE TAYLOR (1783–1824)

Who ran to help me when I fell,
And would some pretty story tell,
Or kiss the place to make it well?
    My mother.

KATHARINE TYNAN (1861–1931)
Irish poet and novelist
In *The Meeting*

As I went up and he came down, my little six-year boy
Upon the stairs we met and kissed, I and my tender Joy.
O fond and true, as lovers do, we kissed and clasped and parted;
And I went up and he went down, refreshed and happy-hearted.

AMANDA VAIL
In *Love Me Little*

'Parents are strange,' Amy said, 'for their age.'

'American girls do have regrets,' Amy said. 'That is what distinguishes them from French girls.'

PETER DE VRIES (*b.* 1910)
American novelist

A suburban mother's role is to deliver children obstetrically once, and by car for ever after.

VITA SACKVILLE-WEST (1892–1962)
British novelist
In Nigel Nicolson's *Portrait of a Marriage*

I know I was cruel to other children because I remember stuffing their nostrils with putty, and beating a little boy with stinging nettles.

KATHARINE WHITEHORN
British journalist
In the *Observer*, 1975

The best careers advice given to the young is 'Find out what you like doing best and get someone to pay you for doing it.'

In *Observations*

Americans, indeed, often seem to be so overwhelmed by their children that they'll do anything for them except stay married to the co-producer.

GRACE WILLIAMS

We learn from experience. A man never wakes up his second baby just to see it smile.

SHIRLEY WILLIAMS (*b.* 1930)
British politician
Quoted in *Daily Mirror*, 2 March 1978

No test tube can breed love and affection. No frozen packet of semen ever read a story to a sleepy child.

NATALIE WOOD (1938–1981)
American film star

The only time a woman really succeeds in changing a man is when he's a baby.

VIRGINIA WOOLF (1882–1941)
British writer
In *Moments of Being*

That great cathedral space which was childhood.

LIFE

ISABELLE ADJANI (*b.* 1955)
French actress
Quoted in *Time*, 1979

Life is worth being lived, but not being discussed all the time.

PRINCESS ANNE (*b.* 1950)

It's a bit of a cliché that the Royal Family leads a sheltered life. It would be true in certain distinct areas, but not in general.

HANNAH ARENDT (1906–1975)
German-American political philosopher

Ideas, as distinguished from events, are never unprecedented.

What I cannot live with may not bother another man's conscience. The result is that conscience will stand against conscience.

Forgiveness is the key to action and freedom.

Nothing and nobody exists on this planet whose very being does not presuppose a spectator. In other words, nothing that is, insofar as it appears, exists in the singular; everything that is is meant to be perceived by somebody. No Man, but men inhabit the earth. Plurality is the law of the earth.

The human condition is such that pain and effort are not just symptoms which can be removed without changing life itself; they are the modes in which life itself, together with the necessity to which it is bound, makes itself felt. For mortals, the 'easy life of the gods' would be a lifeless life.

To expect truth to come from thinking signifies that we mistake the need to think with the urge to know.

JANE AUSTEN (1775–1817)
British novelist
In *Pride and Prejudice*

For what do we live, but to make sport for our neighbours, and laugh at them in our turn?

LAUREN BACALL (*b.* 1924)
American actress

But, Jesus, you can't start worrying about what's *going* to happen. You get spastic enough worrying about what's happening now.

JOAN BAEZ (*b.* 1941)
American folk singer

We (women) have been trained to be impotent.

ENID BAGNOLD (1889–1981)
British writer
In *The Loved and the Envied*

It's not the party of life in the end that's important. It's the comment in the bedroom.

FAITH BALDWIN (1893–1978)
American writer
In *Harvest of Hope*, 1962

Character builds slowly, but it can be torn down again with incredible swiftness.

TALLULAH BANKHEAD (1902–1968)
American film star

We're all paid off in the end, and the fools first.

SYBILLE BEDFORD (*b.* 1911)
British writer
Quoted in *Esquire*, 1964

A part, a large part, of travelling is an engagement of the ego against the world. The world is hydra-headed, as old as the rocks and as changing as the sea . . . the ego wants to arrive at places safely and on time.

To compress, to shape, to label the erratic sequences of life is the perennial function of the judges.

MADEMOISELLE BERTIN (1744–1813)

There is nothing new except that which is forgotten.

ELIZABETH BIBESCO (*d.* 1945)
British novelist

It is never any good dwelling on goodbyes. It is not the being together that it prolongs, it is the parting.

ROSE ELIZABETH BIRD (*b.* 1936)
First woman Chief Justice of California

We have probed the earth, excavated it, burned it, ripped things from it, buried things in it. . . . That does not fit my definition of a good tenant. If we were here on a month-to-month basis, we would have been evicted long ago.

ELIZABETH BOWEN (1899–1973)
Anglo-Irish writer
In *The House in Paris*

Fate is not an eagle, it creeps like a rat.

In *The Death of the Heart*

People are made alarming by one's dread of their unremitting, purposeful continuity.

For people who live on expectations, to face up to their realization is something of an ordeal.

MARJORIE BOWEN
'Sayings of the Week' (*Observer*)

The smart new cliché of the moment usually masks something that was discussed threadbare in the streets of Ur.

LOUISE BROOKS (*b.* 1900)
American actress
Quoted in Kenneth Tynan's 'Profile', *New Yorker*, 11 June 1979

I never gave away anything without wishing I had kept it; nor kept anything without wishing I had given it away.

HELEN GURLEY BROWN (*b.* 1922)
American journalist
Quoted in *Esquire*, 1970

Self-help . . . that is my whole credo. You cannot sit around like a cupcake asking other people to eat you up and discover your great sweetness and charm. You've got to make yourself more cupcakeable all the time, so that you're a better cupcake to be gobbled up.

PEARL S. BUCK (1892–1973)
American novelist
In *What America Means to Me*

Men would rather be starving and free than fed in bonds.

There is, of course, a difference between what one seizes and what one really possesses.

The main barrier between East and West today is that the white man is not willing to give up his superiority and the coloured man is no longer willing to endure his inferiority.

It is not healthy when a nation lives within a nation, as coloured Americans are living inside America. A nation cannot live confident of its tomorrow if its refugees are among its own citizens.

In *To My Daughters, with Love*

Praise out of season, or tactlessly bestowed, can freeze the heart as much as blame.

You cannot make yourself feel something you do not feel, but you can make yourself do right in spite of your feelings.

In *A Bridge for Passing*

All things are possible until they are proved impossible – and even the impossible may only be so as of now.

DAME IVY COMPTON-BURNETT (1892–1969)
English novelist
Quoted in *The Guardian*

Real life seems to have no plots.

In *The Mighty and Their Fall*

There are different kinds of wrong. The people sinned against are not always the best.

RACHEL CARSON (1907–1965)
American scientific writer

Under the philosophy that now seems to guide our destinies, nothing must get in the way of the man with the spray gun.

There can be no double standard. We cannot have peace among men whose hearts find delight in killing any living creature.

ROSALYNN CARTER (*b.* 1927)
Wife of 39th President of the United States

People are the same most everywhere you go . . . They just make their living in different ways.

WILLA CATHER (1873–1947)
American poet
In *O Pioneers*

I like trees because they seem more resigned to the way they have to live than other things do.

EDNAH D. CHENEY
In *Louisa May Alcott, Her Life, Letters and Journals*

Now I am beginning to live a little and feel less like a sick oyster at low tide.

She [Louisa May Alcott] resolved to take fate by the throat and shake a living out of her.

JULIA CHILD (*b.* 1912)
American cookery writer and television performer

Life itself is the proper binge.

JILL CLAYBURGH
American actress

Nothing is inherently valueless. It depends on how far it goes and what the intent is.

COLETTE (Sidonie-Gabrielle) (1873–1954)
French writer

The wily lunatic is lost if through the narrowest crack he allows a sane eye to peer into his locked universe and thus profane it.

Smokers, male and female, inject and excuse idleness in their lives every time they light a cigarette.

JUDY COLLINS (*b.* 1939)
American folk singer

Keeping up with the times is just a matter of living every day.

SHIRLEY CONRAN
British writer
In *Superwoman*

First things first, second things never.

JILLY COOPER (*b.* 1937)
British journalist
'Sayings of the Week' (*Observer*, 24 April 1977)

People who are anti-dog are anti-sex.

MARIE CURIE (1867–1934)
Polish scientist

Nothing in life is to be feared. It is only to be understood.

JOAN DIDION (*b.* 1934)
American writer

Self-respect . . . is a question of recognizing that anything worth having has its price.

MARY DOUGLAS (*b.* 1921)
British writer

Where there is dirt there is system. Dirt is the by-product of a systematic ordering and classification of matter.

ELAINE DUNDY (*b.* 1937)
American writer
In *The Dud Avocado*

Make voyages. Attempt them. That's all there is.

I was merely a disinterested spectator at the Banquet of Life.

GEORGE ELIOT (Marian Evans) (1819–1880)
British novelist

Hatred is like fire; it makes even light rubbish deadly.

Watch your own speech, and notice how it is guided by your less conscious purposes.

Ignorance is not so damnable as humbug, but when it prescribes pills it may happen to do more harm.

To get an idea of our fellow countrymen's miseries, we have only to take a look at their pleasures.

In *Silas Marner*

Nothing is so good as it seems beforehand.

In *Middlemarch*

If we had keen vision and feeling of all ordinary human life, it would be like hearing the grass grow and the squirrel's heart beat, and we should die of that roar which lies on the other side of silence.

In *Adam Bede*

It's them as take advantage that get advantage i' this world.

RALPH WALDO EMERSON (1803–1882)
American writer

Women, as most susceptible, are the best index of the coming hour.

ENGLISH PROVERB

All are good maids, but whence come the bad wives?

BARBARA ETTORE
Quoted in *Harper's Magazine*, 1974

Ettore's Observation: The other line (queue) always moves faster.

DAME EDITH EVANS (1888–1976)
British actress
Quoted in *Sunday Times*, 1961

Life is long enough, it seems to me, but not quite broad enough. Things crowd in so thickly it takes time for experience to become clarified before it can be placed to the full service of art.

MARIANNE FAITHFULL (*b.* 1947)
British actress and rock singer

The seventies were a desert for me – I really couldn't get it together until very recently.

We really believed, because we were so young, that anything was possible. We had enormous confidence. We believed we'd come out of it all okay . . . You see, you always think it won't be you.

F. SCOTT FITZGERALD (1896–1940)
American writer
In Grace Kellogg's *The Two Lives of Edith Wharton*

On meeting Edith Wharton
Mrs Wharton, do you know what's the matter with you? You don't know anything about life.

MARJORIE FLEMING (1803–1811)
British child poet and diarist
In *Journal*

I am going to turn over a new life and am going to be a very good girl and be obedient to Isa Keith, here there is plenty of gooseberries which makes my teeth watter.

JANET FRAME (*b.* 1924)
New Zealand writer

'For your own good' is a persuasive argument that will eventually make man agree to his own destruction.

MARGARET FULLER (1810–1850)
American author and critic

For precocity some great price is always demanded sooner or later in life.

LOIS GOLD

Life is the only sentence which doesn't end with a period.

CELIA GREEN
In *The Decline and Fall of Science* ('Aphorisms')

The remarkable thing about the human kind is its range of limitations.

BARBARA GOGAN
Rock singer (*The Passions*)

There's nothing I enjoy more than being on stage and slagging men off.

JOYCE GRENFELL (1910–1980)
British comedienne
'Sayings of the Week' (*Observer*, 12 September 1976)

There is no such thing as the pursuit of happiness, but there is the discovery of joy.

MARGARET HALSEY (*b.* 1910)
American writer
In *With Malice Toward Some*

Humility is not my forte, and whenever I dwell for any length of time on my own shortcomings, they gradually begin to seem mild, harmless, rather engaging little things, not at all like the staring defects in other people's characters.

DEBBIE HARRY (*b.* 1941)
American rock singer

If I read anything cruel I have to have a couple of days to get over it. If it came at me all the time I'd go round throwing acid into people's faces.

I manage to look so young because I am mentally retarded. I think the reason I don't look as I really am is because of the junk and the yoga. I'm not a Communist, I'm a Humanist. That's why I'm attracted to Lenin.

JACQUETTA HAWKES (*b.* 1910)
British archaeologist
Quoted in *New Statesman*, January 1957

The only inequalities that matter begin in the mind. It is not income levels but differences in mental equipment that keep people apart, breed feelings of inferiority.

LILLIAN HELLMAN (*b.* 1907)
American playwright

I do not believe in recovery. The past, with its pleasures, its rewards, its foolishness, its punishments, is there for each of us for ever, and it should be.

Callous greed grows pious very fast.

KATHARINE HEPBURN (*b.* 1909)
American actress

Discipline is the basis of a satisfying life, but discipline is out of style.

BILLIE HOLIDAY (1915–1959)
American blues singer

I've been told that nobody sings the word 'hunger' like I do.

ELLEN STURGIS HOOPER (1816–1841)
In *Life a Duty*

I slept, and dreamed that life was Beauty;
I woke, and found that life was Duty.

HELEN HOOVER
In *The Long-Shadowed Forest*, ('The Waiting Hills') 1963

The natural world is dynamic. From the expanding universe to the hair on a baby's head, nothing is the same from now to the next moment.

MARION HOWARD

Life is like a blanket too short. You pull it up and your toes rebel, you yank it down and shivers meander about your shoulder; but cheerful folks manage to draw their knees up and pass a very comfortable night.

JULIA WARD HOWE (1819–1910)
Hymn writer
In *Battle Hymn of the American Republic*

Mine eyes have seen the glory of the coming of the Lord:
He is trampling out the vintage where the grapes of wrath are stored.

VIRGINIA CARY HUDSON
In *O Ye Jigs and Juleps!*

Education is what you learn in books, and nobody knows you know it but your teacher.

MAHALIA JACKSON
American blues singer

Anybody singing the blues is in a deep pit yelling for help.

PAMELA HANSFORD JOHNSON (1912–1981)
British writer
In *Cork Street Next to the Hatter's*

Dorothy, like a good many bad-tempered people, was quick to forgive affronts, so that she could start giving and receiving them again.

JANIS JOPLIN (1943–1970)
American rock singer

You can destroy your now by worrying about tomorrow.

I am here to have a party, man, as best as I can while I'm on this earth. I think that's your duty too.

All my life I just wanted to be a beatnik, meet all the heavies, get stoned, get laid, have a good time. That's all I ever wanted, except I knew I had a good voice and could always get a couple of beers off it. All of a sudden someone threw me in this rock 'n' roll band . . . I decided then and there, that was it. I never wanted to do anything else. It was better than with any man, y'know. Maybe that's the trouble . . .

HELEN KELLER (1880–1968)
Writer and lecturer (born deaf and blind)

Although the world is very full of suffering, it is also full of the overcoming of it.

Toleration . . . is the greatest gift of the mind; it requires the same effort of the brain that it takes to balance oneself on a bicycle.

The highest result of education is tolerance.

The heresy of one age becomes the orthodoxy of the next.

In *Helen Keller's Journal*, 1938
Few pleasures there are indeed without an aftertouch of pain, but that is the preservation which keeps them sweet.

Character cannot be developed in ease and quiet. Only through experience of trial and suffering can the soul be strengthened, vision cleared, ambition inspired, and success achieved.

In *We Bereaved*

Instead of comparing our lot with that of those who are more fortunate than we are, we should compare it with the lot of the great majority of our fellow men. It then appears that we are among the privileged.

In *Out of the Dark*, 1913

When we do the best that we can, we never know what miracle is wrought in our life, or in the life of another.

In *The Image*

How I wish that all men would take sunrise for their slogan and leave the shadow of sunset behind.

JEAN KERR (*b.* 1923)
American writer

Do you know how helpless you feel if you have a full cup of coffee in your hand and you start to sneeze?

CAMILLA KOFFLER

I tend to be suspicious of people whose love of animals is exaggerated; they are often frustrated in their relationships with humans.

ANN LANDERS (*b.* 1918)
American journalist

Trouble is the common denominator of living. It is the great equaliser.

DOROTHEA LANGE (1885–1965)
American photographer
In N. Lyons' *Photographers on Photography*

On my darkroom door for many years I had posted the words of Francis Bacon: 'The contemplation of things as they are, without substitution or imposture, without error or confusion, is in itself a nobler thing than a whole harvest of invention.'

SUZANNE K. LANGER (*b.* 1895)
American philospher

A new idea is a light that illuminates presences which simply had no form for us before the light fell on them.

FANNY HEASLIP LEA (*b.* 1884)
In *Fate*

It's odd to think we might have been
Sun, moon and stars unto each other –
Only, I turned down one little street
As you went up another.

FRAN LEBOWITZ (*circa* 1951)
American journalist
In *Metropolitan Life*

Everyone in Milan works and it if rains in Milan they blame it on Rome . . . Nobody in Rome works and if it rains in Rome *and* they happen to notice it they blame it on Milan.

There is no such thing as inner peace. There is only nervousness or death. Any attempt to prove otherwise constitutes unacceptable behaviour.

DORIS LESSING (*b.* 1919)
British writer

In university they don't tell you that the greater part of the law is learning to tolerate fools.

There is no one on this earth who is not twisted by fear and insecurity.

ANNE MORROW LINDBERGH (*b.* 1906)
American writer
In *Gift from the Sea*

The most exhausting thing in life, I have discovered, is being insincere.

Duration is not a test of true or false.

The collector walks with blinders on; he sees nothing but the prize. In fact, the acquisitive instinct is incompatible with true appreciation of beauty.

In *The Wave of the Future*

Only in growth, reform, and change, paradoxically enough, is true security to be found.

In *North to the Orient*

If one talks to more than four people, it is an audience; and one cannot really think or exchange thoughts with an audience.

ANITA LOOS (*b.* 1893)
American writer

Memory is more indelible than ink.

LORETTA LYNN
American singer

I've seen things, and that's almost the same as doing them.

MARYA MANNES (*b.* 1904)
American novelist and poet

The suppression of civil liberties is to many less a matter for horror than the curtailment of the freedom to profit.

Flirtation is merely an expression of considered desire coupled with an admission of its impracticability.

ELSA MAXWELL (1883–1963)
American socialite

Some said that life is a party. You join after it's started and you leave before it's finished.

ELAINE MAY (*b.* 1932)
American actress and writer
Quoted by Gore Vidal in *New Statesman*, 4 May 1973

I like a moral issue so much more than a real issue.

MARY MCCARTHY (*b.* 1912)
American writer
In *On the Contrary*

Modern neurosis began with the discoveries of Copernicus.

Science made man feel small by showing him that the earth was not the centre of the universe.

Life for the European is a career; for the American, it is a hazard.

We are a nation of twenty million bathrooms, with a humanist in every tub.

It is true that America produces and consumes more cars, soap, and bathtubs than any other nation, but we live among these objects, rather than by them.

The happy ending is our national belief.

The mark of the historic is the nonchalance with which it picks up an individual and deposits him in a trend, like a house playfully moved in a tornado.

There are no new truths, but only truths that have not been recognised by those who have perceived them without noticing.

PHYLLIS MCGINLEY (*b.* 1905)
In *The Province of the Heart*

People are no longer sinful, they are only immature or under-privileged or frightened or, more particularly, sick.

This is the gist of what I know
Give advice and buy a foe.

HELEN MACINNES (*b.* 1907)
American novelist

Nothing is interesting if you're not interested.

RUTH MCKENNEY (1911–1972)
American writer

Man has no nobler function than to defend the truth.

MIGNON MCLAUGHLIN
American writer

The head never rules the heart, but just becomes its partner in crime.

We're all born brave, trusting and greedy, and most of us remain greedy.

It's innocence when it charms us, ignorance when it doesn't.

Our strength is often composed of the weakness we're damned if we're going to show.

MARGARET MEAD (1901–1978)
American anthropologist

Pigs and cows and chickens and people are all competing for grain.

What's happening now is an immigration in time, with people over forty the migrants into the present age, and the children born in it the natives.

EDNA ST VINCENT MILLAY (1892–1950)
American poet

Evil alone has oil for every wheel.

It is not true that life is one damn thing after another – it's one damn thing over and over.

EDITH MIRRIELEES
American writer

Experience shows that exceptions are as true as rules.

JONI MITCHELL (*b.* 1943)
Canadian singer

When I was two feet off the ground I collected broken glass and cats. When I was three feet off the ground I made drawings of animals and forest fires. When I was four feet off the ground I discovered boys and bicycles.

MARIA MONTESSORI (1870–1952)
Italian educator

Discipline must come through liberty . . . We do not consider an individual disciplined when he has been rendered as artificially silent as a mute and as immovable as a paralytic. He is an individual *annihilated*, not disciplined.

IRIS MURDOCH (*b.* 1919)
British philosopher and novelist

Philosophy . . . means looking at things which one takes for granted and suddenly seeing that they are very odd indeed.

MADAME NECKER
Wife of French statesman Jacques Necker (1732–1824)

Fortune does not change men: it unmasks them.

LOUISE NEVELSON
American photographer
Quoted in *Newsweek*, 4 February 1974

What we call reality is an agreement that people have arrived at to make life more liveable.

KATHLEEN NORRIS (1900–1966)
American novelist

Life is easier to take than you'd think: all that is necessary is to accept the impossible, do without the indispensable and bear the intolerable.

CAROLINE E. S. NORTON (1808–1877)
In *Not Lost But Gone Before*

For death and life, in ceaseless strife,
  Beat wild on this world's shore,
And all our calm is in that balm –
  Not lost but gone before.

KATHERINE NOTT
British writer
In *Contemporary Novelists*, 1976

If philosophy interferes with life, give up philosophy.

EDNA O'BRIEN (*b.* 1936)
Irish writer

When anyone asks me about the Irish character, I say look at the trees. Maimed, stark and misshapen, but ferociously tenacious. The Irish have got gab but are too touchy to be humorous. Me too.

GRACE PALEY (*b.* 1922)
American writer

Art is too long and life is too short.

DOROTHY PARKER (1893–1967)
American writer and wit
In *Enough Rope*

Travel, trouble, music, art,
A kiss, a frock, a rhyme, –
I never said they feed my heart,
But still, they pass my time.

In *Enough Rope* ('The Veteran')

Inertia rides and riddles me:
The which is called Philosophy.

In *Sunset Gun* ('Fair Weather')

They sicken of the calm, who know the storm.

IRENE PETER

Ignorance is no excuse – it's the real thing.

Living is entirely too time-consuming.

MARY PETTIBONE POOLE

Culture is what your butcher would have if he were a surgeon.

IVY BAKER PRIEST
In *Parade*, 16 February 1958

The world is round and the place which may seem like the end may also be only the beginning.

AGNES REPPLIER (1858–1950)
American essayist

There are few nudities so objectionable as the naked truth.

JOAN RIVERS (*b.* 1935)
American comedienne

Who fits in any more? I was invited to a pot party and I brought Tupperware.

LINDA RONSTADT (*b.* 1946)
American rock singer

I'm a survivor. Being a survivor doesn't mean you have to be made out of steel and it doesn't mean you have to be ruthless. It means you are basically on your own side and you want to win.

ELEANOR ROOSEVELT (1884–1962)
Wife of 32nd President of the United States
In *Autobiography*

Life was meant to be lived and curiosity must be kept alive. One must never, for whatever reason, turn his back on life.

DIANA ROSS (*b.* 1944)
American singer

You can only live one dream at a time.

MARGARET LEE RUNBECK

Happiness is not a state to arrive at, but a manner of travelling.

GEORGES SAND (1804–1876)
French writer
In *Mauprat*

We cannot tear out a single page from our life, but we can throw the whole book into the fire.

MARIA SCHELL
Quoted in *Time*, 3 March 1958

Peace is when time doesn't matter as it passes by.

DIANE B. SCHULDER (*b.* 1937)
American lawyer
In Robin Morgan's *Sisterhood is Powerful*

Law is a reflection and a source of prejudice. It both enforces and suggests forms of bias.

MARTHA SCOTT

Don't make the mistake of treating your dogs like humans, or they'll treat you like dogs.

DAME EDITH SITWELL (1887–1964)
British poet

Everybody is somebody's bore.

GRACE SLICK (*b.* 1939)
American rock singer

In the 1960s everybody took drugs to expand their consciousness. In the 1970s they took them to get rid of it.

LILLIAN SMITH (1897–1966)
American writer

Education is a private matter between the person and the world of knowledge and experience, and has little to do with school or college.

PATTI SMITH (*b.* 1946)
American rock singer

While I'm very intelligent, I'm no intellectual. All my beliefs, political and otherwise, are very romantic. It's like me having a crush on Prince Charles. I don't know anything about him. I just think there's something sexy about him.

I'm equal parts Brando and Ballenciaga.

After all I *am* the last white nigger.

STEVIE SMITH (1902–1971)
British poet

In *Recognition Not Enough*

Sin recognised – but that – may keep us humble.
But oh, it keeps us nasty.

SUSAN SONTAG (*b.* 1933)
American essayist
'On Photography'

Humankind lingers unregenerately in Plato's cave, still revelling, its age-old habit, in mere images of the truth.

All possibility of understanding is rooted in the ability to say no.

On 'Styles of Radical Will'

Existence is no more than the precarious attainment of relevance in an intensely mobile flux of the past, present and future.

Depression is melancholy minus its charms.

In *Against Interpretation* ('The Anthropologist as Hero')

The felt unreliability of human experience brought about by the inhuman acceleration of historical change has led every sensitive modern mind to the recording of some kind of nausea, of intellectual vertigo.

In *Against Interpretation* ('Notes on Camp')

If tragedy is an experience of hyper-involvement, comedy is an experience of under-involvement, of detachment.

In *Partisan Review*

The white race is the cancer of human history. It is the white race, and it alone, its ideologies and inventions, which eradicate autonomous civilizations wherever it spreads. It has upset the ecological balance of the planet which now threatens the very existence of life itself.

HILDE SPIEL

Malice is like a game of poker or tennis; you don't play it with anyone who is manifestly inferior to you.

MADAME DE STAËL (1766–1817)
French writer

To understand all is to forgive all.

GERTRUDE STEIN (1874–1946)
American writer

Two things are always the same, the dance and war. One might say anything is the same but the dance and war are particularly the same because one can see them. That is what they are for.

BETTY TALMADGE
Divorced wife of Senator Herman Talmadge

Life is what happens to you when you're making other plans.

SARA TEASDALE (1884–1933)
American poet
In *At Midnight*

Now at last I have come to see what life is,
Nothing is ever ended, everything only begun,
And the brave victories that seem so splendid
Are never really won.

In *Wisdom*

What we have never had, remains;
It is the things we have that go.

In *The Philosopher*

I make the most of all that comes,
And the least of all that goes.

AMANDA VAIL
In *Love Me Little*

We talked a lot about life. There was nothing else to talk about.

ABIGAIL VAN BUREN (*b.* 1918)
American writer and journalist

People who fight fire with fire usually end up with ashes.

MARY WEBB (1882–1927)
British novelist
In *Precious Bane*

It made me gladsome to be getting some education, it being like a big window opening.

PHYLLIS WEBB (*b.* 1927)
Canadian poet

To contemplate suicide is surely the best exercise of the imagination.

SIMONE WEIL (1909–1943)
French writer and philosopher

Death and labour are things of necessity and not of choice. The world only gives itself to Man in the form of food and warmth if Man gives himself to the world in the form of labour. But death and labour can be submitted to either in an attitude of revolt or in one of consent. They can be submitted to in their naked truth or else wrapped around with lies.

A hurtful act is the transference to others of the degradation which we bear in ourselves.

We do not acquire humility. There is humility in us – only we humiliate ourselves before false gods.

Algebra and money are essentially levellers; the first intellectually, the second effectively.

We have to endure the discordance between imaginition and fact. It is better to say, 'I am suffering', than to say 'This landscape is ugly'.

The same suffering is much harder to bear for a high motive than for a base one. The people who stood motionless, from one to eight in the morning, for the sake of having an egg, would have found it very difficult to do in order to save a human life.

All sins are attempts to fill voids.

Justice: to be ever ready to admit that another person is something quite different from what we read when he is there or when we think about him. Or, rather, to read in him that he is certainly something different, perhaps something completely different, from what we read in him. Every being cries out to be read differently.

MAE WEST (1882–1980)
American film star

When choosing between two evils, I always like to try the one I've never tried before.

DAME REBECCA WEST (1892–1983)
British writer

'Sayings of the Week' (*Observer*, 7 September 1975)

You couldn't live eighty-two years in the world without being disillusioned.

In Peter Wolfe's *Rebecca West: Artist and Thinker*

Man is a hating rather than a loving animal.

Man does not want to know. When he knows very little he plays with the possibilities of knowledge, but when he finds that the pieces he has been putting together are going to spell out the answer he is frightened and he throws them in every direction; and another civilization falls.

In *The Court and the Castle*

Humanity is never more sphinx-like than when it is expressing itself.

VITA SACKVILLE-WEST (1892–1962)
British writer

I have come to the conclusion, after many years of sometimes sad experience, that you cannot come to any conclusion at all.

EDITH WHARTON (1862–1937)
American novelist
In *Xingu*

Mrs Ballinger is one of the ladies who pursue Culture in bands, as though it were dangerous to meet it alone.

VIRGINIA WOOLF (1882–1941)
British writer
In *A Writer's Diary*

If we didn't live venturously, plucking the wild goat by the beard, and trembling over precipices, we should never be depressed, I've no doubt; but already should be faded, fatalistic and aged.

In Kenneth Tynan's *Curtains* (Definition of a highbrow)

A man or woman of thoroughbred intelligence galloping across open country in pursuit of an idea.

SOCIETY

ABIGAIL ADAMS (1744–1818)
American letter writer, wife of U.S. President John Adams.

If particular care and attention is not paid to the ladies we are determined to foment a rebellion and will not hold ourselves bound by any laws in which we have no voice or representation.

We have too many high-sounding words and too few actions that correspond with them.

RENATA ADLER
In *Speedboat*, 1976

Idle people are often bored, and bored people, unless they sleep a lot, are cruel.

It is always self-defeating to pretend to the style of a generation younger than your own; it simply erases your own experience in history.

ANAHARIO
Wife of Grey Owl

Any interference with nature is damnable. Not only nature but also the people will suffer.

HANNAH ARENDT (1906–1975)
German-American political philosopher

The fault is in us.

DAISY ASHFORD
In *The Young Visiters* (written when she was fourteen)

Here I am tied down to this life he said . . . being royal has many painfull drawbacks.

I am very fond of fresh air and royalties.

MYRA BARKER

A science career for women is now almost as acceptable as being cheerleader.

CECIL BEATON (1904–1980)
British photographer and designer
On romantic novelist Elinor Glyn

Mrs Glyn achieved the paradox of bringing not only 'good taste' to the colony [Hollywood], but also 'sex appeal'. She coined the word 'It', and taught Rudolf Valentino to kiss the palm of a lady's hand rather than its back.

SIMONE DE BEAUVOIR (*b.* 1908)
French writer
In *Pour une morale de l'ambiguité*

The misfortune which befalls man from his once having been a child is that his liberty was at first concealed from him, and all his life he will retain the nostalgia for a time when he was ignorant of its exigencies.

Humanity is something more than a mere species – it is a historical development.

RUTH BENEDICT (1887–1948)
American anthropologist

Society in its full sense . . . is never an entity separable from the individuals who compose it.

MARILYN BERGER
In *Washington Week in Review*, 19 December 1975

Power is what it's perceived to be.

ELIZABETH BOWEN (1899–1973)
Anglo-Irish writer
In *The Death of the Heart*

It is not our exalted feelings, it is our sentiments that build the necessary home.

In *The House in Paris*

Meeting people unlike oneself does not enlarge one's outlook; it only confirms one's idea that one is unique.

Young girls like the excess of any quality. Without knowing, they want to suffer, to suffer they must exaggerate; they like to have loud chords struck on them.

PEARL S. BUCK (1892–1973)
American novelist
In *What America Means to Me*

It is natural anywhere that people like their own kind, but it is not necessarily natural that their fondness for their own kind should lead them to the subjection of whole groups of other people not like them.

Every great mistake has a halfway moment, a split second when it can be recalled and perhaps remedied.

In *To My Daughters, With Love*

To eat bread without hope is still slowly to starve to death.

Growth itself contains the germ of happiness.

MRS PATRICK CAMPBELL (1865–1940)
British actress

An eminent biologist spent an entire dinner talking to Mrs Patrick Campbell about ants.

'They have their own army and their own police force!'

'Indeed,' said Mrs Patrick Campbell. 'No navy?'

HORTENSE CALISHER (*b.* 1911)
American novelist
Quoted in *New York Times* 19 September 1977

Sociology, the guilty science, functions best by alarm.

JESSE CARR
Quoted in *Newsweek*, 27 September 1976

Being powerful is like being a lady. If you have to tell people you are, you ain't.

COCO CHANEL (Gabrielle) (1883–1971)
French couturière

He who does not enjoy his own company is usually right.

M. Haedrich's *Coco Chanel – Her Life, Her Secrets*

Silence is the cruelty of the provincial.

RUTH COHEN
Principal, Newnham College, Cambridge
'Sayings of the Week' (*Observer*, 3 October 1971)

Co-education is unutterably unimportant.

COLETTE (Sidonie-Gabrielle) (1873–1954)
French writer
In *Earthly Paradise*

There is nothing that gives more assurance than a mask.

Humility has its origin in an awareness of unworthiness, and sometimes too in a dazzled awareness of saintliness.

ELIZABETH DREW
American writer

Propaganda . . . is a seeding of the self in the consciousness of others.

ELAINE DUNDY (*b.* 1937)
American writer

I find I always have to write something on a steamed mirror.

MEL ELFIN (*b.* 1893)
Quoted in *Newsweek*, 20 January 1969

In a romantic nation such as this, where soap opera, Mother's Day and June Allyson were invented, the power to inspire, not the power to command, is the most potent tool of Presidential leadership.

GEORGE ELIOT (Marian Evans) (1819–1880)
British novelist
In *Daniel Deronda*

The strongest principle of growth lies in human choice.

QUEEN ELIZABETH II (*b.* 1926)

True patriotism doesn't exclude an understanding of the patriotism of others.

ANNA FREUD (1895–1982)
Austrian-English psychologist and daughter of Sigmund Freud

Creative minds always have been known to survive any kind of bad training.

DOROTHY FULDHEIM (*b.* 1893)
In *A Thousand Friends*

This is a youth-oriented society, and the joke is on them because youth is a disease from which we all recover.

MARGARET FULLER (1810–1850)
American author and critic
In *Summer on the Lakes*

The civilized man is a larger mind but a more imperfect nature than the savage.

HANNAH FLAGG GOULD (1789–1865)
In *The Wheatfield*

Wisdom, Power and Goodness meet
In the bounteous field of wheat.

RÉMY DE GOURMONT (1858–1915)
French poet and novelist

What is truly indispensable for the conduct of life has been taught us by women – the small rules of courtesy, the actions that win us the warmth or deference of others; the words that assure us a welcome; the attitudes that must be varied to mesh with character or situation; all social strategy. It is listening to women that teaches us to speak to men.

MARGARET HALSEY (*b.* 1910)
American writer
In *With Malice Toward Some*

The attitude of the English towards English history reminds one a good deal of the attitude of a Hollywood director towards love.

The English never smash in a face. They merely refrain from asking it to dinner.

DEBBIE HARRY (*b.* 1941)
American rock singer
On Los Angeles

Yuk! This placc is onc big parking lot – it's like walking through an endless supermarket.

JACQUETTA HAWKES (*b.* 1910)
British archaeologist

The discouragement of radical thought must lead to the closed society and closed mind – Catholicism through its liking for ignorance; Protestantism through its approval of money making, respectability and the whole drowned and mitred body of the status quo.

FRANCES HAWKINS
In *Youth's Behaviour*, 1663

Being set at the table, scratch not thyself, and take thou heed as much as thou can'st to spit, cough and blow at thy nose; but if it be needful, do it dexterously without much noise, turning thy face sideling.

VIRGINIA CARY HUDSON
In *O Ye Jigs and Juleps!*

Etiquette is what you are doing and saying when people are looking and listening. What you are thinking is your business.

BARBARA A. HUFF
Quoted in *New York Times*, 26 May 1974

The two places one should always go first class are in hospitals and on ships.

ADA LOUISE HUXTABLE
American writer and critic

Real estate is the closest thing to the proverbial pot of gold.

ELIZABETH JANEWAY (*b.* 1913)
American writer
On power

It is . . . the ability not to have to please.

HELEN KELLER (1880–1968)
Writer and lecturer (born deaf and blind)
In *Optimism*

No loss by flood and lightning, no destruction of cities and temples by the hostile forces of nature, has deprived man of so many noble lives and impulses as those which his intolerance has destroyed.

CAROLINE KELLY
Australian anthropologist

We give people a box in the suburbs, it's called a house, and every night they sit in it staring at another box; in the morning they run off to another box, called an office; and at the weekends they get into another box, on wheels this time, and grope their way through endless traffic jams.

MARY ELLEN KELLY

Natives who beat drums to drive off evil spirits are objects of scorn to smart Americans who blow horns to break up traffic jams.

LISA KIRK

A gossip is one who talks to you about others; a bore is one who talks to you about himself; and a brilliant conversationalist is one who talks to you about yourself.

FRANCES LANAHAN (*b.* 1921)
American writer
Quoted in *Esquire*, 1965

People who live entirely by the fertility of their imaginations are fascinating, brilliant and often charming. But they should be sat next to at dinner parties, not lived with.

CAROL LAWRENCE
Quoted in *TV Guide*, 17 May 1969

A duchess will be a duchess in a bath towel. It's all a matter of style.

HELEN LAWRENSON
American journalist

The rich only give to the rich.

DORIS LESSING (*b.* 1919)
British writer
In *The Grass is Singing*

When a white man in Africa by accident looks into the eyes of a native and sees the human being (which it is his chief preoccupation to avoid), his sense of guilt, which he denies, fumes up in resentment and he brings down the whip.

ADA LEVERSON (1862–1933)
In *The Limit*

It is an infallible sign of the second-rate in nature and intellect to make use of everything and everyone.

ROSA LEWIS (1867–1952)
British hotelier
In D. Fielding's *The Duchess of Jermyn Street*

I knew him before he was born.

ALICE ROOSEVELT LONGWORTH (1884–1979)
American socialite
To Joseph McCarthy, who addressed her as 'Alice'

The policeman and the trashman may call me Alice. You cannot.

EMILY LOTNEY

A converted cannibal is one who, on Friday, eats only fishermen.

MARYA MANNES (*b.* 1904)
American novelist and poet
In *More in Anger*

The earth we abuse and the living things we kill will, in the end, take their revenge; for in exploiting their presence we are diminishing our future.

People on horses look better than they are. People in cars look worse than they are.

THE DUCHESS OF MARLBOROUGH
'Sayings of the Week' (*Observer*, 26 July 1953)

It's not worth giving dinner parties at Blenheim. The State dining-room is on show, and our dining-room only holds thirty.

SYBIL MARSHALL
In *An Experiment in Education*

Education must have an end in view, for it is not an end in itself.

KARL MARX (1818–1883)
German founder of Communism
Quoted in *Columbia Forum*, Summer 1972

Social progress can be measured with precision by the social position of the female sex.

ELSA MAXWELL (1883–1963)
American socialite
In Stephen Birmingham's *The Right People*

Cocktails are society's most enduring invention.

In *How to Do It*

Anatomize the character of a successful hostess and the knife will lay bare the fact that she owes her position to one of three things: she is liked, or she is feared, or she is important.

MARY MCCARTHY (*b.* 1912)
American writer

Every age has a keyhole to which its eye is pasted.

An unrectified case of injustice has a terrible way of lingering, restlessly, in the social atmosphere like an unfinished question.

MIGNON MCLAUGHLIN
American writer

It's the most unhappy people who most fear change.

If you are brave too often, people will come to expect it of you.

The only courage that matters is the kind that gets you from one moment to the next.

A car is useless in New York, essential everywhere else. The same with good manners.

Every society honours its live conformists and its dead troublemakers.

MERLE L. MEACHAM

In a few minutes a computer can make a mistake so great that it would take many men many months to equal it.

The trouble with being tolerant is that people think you don't understand the problem.

MARGARET MEAD (1901–1978)
American anthropologist

We won't have a society if we destroy the environment.

In almost any society, I think, the quality of the nonconformists is likely to be just as good as, and no better than, that of the conformists.

EVE MERRIAM
In *The Last Laugh*

Mary, Mary
Urban Mary,
How does your sidewalk grow?
With chewing gum wads
With cigarette butts
And popsicle sticks
And potato chip bags
And candy wrappers
And beer cans
And broken bottles
And crusts of pizza
And coffee grounds
And burnt-out light bulbs
And a garbage
    strike all in a row.

AGNES MEYER (1887–1970)
American social worker

From the nineteenth-century view of science as a God, the twentieth century has begun to see it as a devil. It behoves us now to understand that science is neither one nor the other.

JESSICA MITFORD (*b.* 1917)
British writer
In *The American Prison Business*

When is conduct a crime and when is a crime not a crime? When Somebody Up There – a monarch, a dictator, a Pope, a legislator – so decrees.

NANCY MITFORD (1904–1973)
British writer
In L. & M. Cowan's *The Wit of Women*

English women are elegant until they are ten years old, and perfect on grand occasions.

In *The Pursuit of Love*

I was always led to suppose that no educated person spoke of notepaper.

MARIANNE MOORE (1887–1972)
American poet
In *Silence*

My father used to say
'Superior people never make long visits.'

MURIEL OXENBERG MURPHY
Quoted in *New York Times*, 23 July 1976

Social life is a form of do-it-yourself theatre.

LAURA NADER
American writer
In *No Access To Law*

The law is a business whose outlook is shared by its major clients.

Quoted in *Newsweek*, 20 July 1970

Anthropologists may go all over the world, only to discover that the most bizarre culture is the one they started from.

DOROTHY NEVILL

The real art of conversation is not only to say the right thing in the right place but to leave unsaid the wrong thing at the tempting moment.

FLORENCE NIGHTINGALE (1820–1910)
Nursing pioneer
In her diary, quoted in *Eminent Victorians*

A profession, a trade, a necessary occupation, something to fill and employ all my faculties, I have always felt essential to me . . . The first thought I can remember and the last was nursing work . . . Everything has been tried, foreign travel, kind friends, everything. My God! What is to become of me? . . . In my thirty-first year, I see nothing but death.

ISABEL PATERSON
In *The God of the Machine*

The humanitarian wishes to be a prime mover in the lives of others. He cannot admit either the divine or the natural order by which men have the power to help themselves.

IRENE PETER

Just because everything is different doesn't mean anything has changed.

MARIE-FRANCE PISIER
Quoted in *Newsweek*, 16 May 1977

People wear resort clothes, but actually Hollywood is an enormous factory.

DIANE DE POITIERS (1499–1566)

Calumny is like counterfeit money: many people who would not coin it circulate it without qualms.

SALLY QUINN

To understand a society it is essential to understand how people climb. If there are more than two people together, if there are three, one of them is climbing.

AGNES REPPLIER (1858–1950)
American essayist
In *Are Americans Timid?*

A world of vested interests is not a world which welcomes the disruptive force of candour.

ELEANOR ROOSEVELT (1884–1962)
Wife of 32nd President of the United States

Remember, no one can make you feel inferior without your consent.

EDNA G. ROSTOW

Everyone is the child of his past.

DOROTHY L. SAYERS (1893–1957)
British author

The keeping of an idle woman is a badge of superior social status.

GEORGE BERNARD SHAW (1856–1950)
Irish playwright
In Stephen Winston's *Days with Bernard Shaw*
On Ellen Terry

She was an extremely beautiful girl and as innocent as a rose. When Watts kissed her, she took for granted she was going to have a baby.

CORNELIA OTIS SKINNER (1901–1979)
American actress

A hundred years from now, I dare say, some dreamy collector will pay a cool thousand for an old milk bottle, and I wish I had the equivalent for what my hot-water bag will bring in 2034. Why we should be so beguiled by the antique is a riddle that perhaps only the interior decorator can solve.

GRACE SLICK (*b.* 1939)
American rock singer

It's a bit difficult to get hippies organized into anything.

SYDNEY SMITH (1771–1845)
British clergyman and writer
In Lady S. Holland's *Memoir*, 1855

There are three sexes – men, women and clergymen.

SOCRATES (496–406 BC)
Greek philosopher

Once made equal to man, woman becomes his superior.

SUSAN SONTAG (*b.* 1933)
American essayist
In *Death Kit*

He who despises himself esteems himself as a self-despiser.

In *Styles of Radical Will*

It doesn't seem inaccurate to say more people in this society who aren't actively made are, at best, reformed or potential lunatics.

SPANISH PROVERB

To tell a woman what she may not do is to tell her what she can.

MADAME DE STAËL (1766–1817)
French writer
In *Delphine*

A man must know how to brave public opinion, a woman how to submit to it.

ELIZABETH CADY STANTON (1815–1902)
American suffragette

Social science affirms that a woman's place in society marks the level of civilization.

GLORIA STEINEM (*b.* 1934)
American feminist

Law and justice are not always the same. When they aren't, destroying the law may be the first step towards changing it.

LADY SUMMERSKILL (1901–1980)
British politician
Quoted in the *Observer*, 1960

Nagging is the repetition of unpalatable truths.

LILY TOMLIN (*b.* 1939)
American comedienne

There's so much plastic in this culture that vinyl leopardskin is becoming an endangered synthetic.

ELSA TRIOLET (1896–1970)
French writer

To be a prophet it's sufficient to be a pessimist.

BARBARA TUCHMAN (*b.* 1912)
American historian
In *The Guns of August*

War is the unfolding of miscalculations.

GRACE VANDERBILT
In consolation for being preceded by Nancy Astor at a dinner given by Theodore Roosevelt

The Astors skinned skunks a hundred years before the Vanderbilts worked ferries.

SIMONE WEIL (1909–1943)
French writer

Unless protected by an armour of lies, man cannot endure might without suffering a blow in the depth of his soul.

KATHARINE WHITEHORN
British journalist
In the *Observer*, 1973

They should stop calling it 'Social Security'. It's as secure as a cardboard raft.

WOMEN'S INSTITUTE
Quoted in Simon Goodenough's *Jam and Jerusalem*

When the Women's Institute started at the turn of the century, they were determined to cross class barriers. One president reported with satisfaction: 'We have done very well: we have elected five ladies, five women and one school teacher.'

LADY WOOTTON (*b.* 1897)
British politician
'Sayings of the Week' (*Observer*)

Two hundred years ago we made a practice of treating lunatics as criminals. Nowadays we are more inclined to treat criminals as lunatics.

ELIZABETH WORDSWORTH (1840–1932)
British University College principal

If all the good people were clever
And all clever people were good.
The world would be nicer than ever
We thought that it possibly could.

YIDDISH PROVERB

The girl who can't dance says the band can't play.

FRAU EVA VON ZEPPELIN
On rock group Led Zeppelin

They may be world famous but four shrieking monkeys are not going to use a privileged family name without permission.

FRIENDSHIP AND LONELINESS

JANE ACE (1905–1974)
American writer

Marge and I are insufferable friends.

JANE AUSTEN (1775–1817)
British novelist
In *Emma*

Business, you know, may bring money, but friendship hardly ever does.

Those who do not complain are never pitied.

MYRTLE BARKER
In *I Am Only One*, 1966

People fighting their aloneness will do almost anything to avoid silence.

UGO BETTI (1892–1954)
Italian playwright
In *The Gambler*

Sisterly love is, of all sentiments, the most abstract. Nature does not grant it any functions.

THE BIBLE
In *Book of Ruth* 1:16
The widow Ruth to her mother-in-law

Whither thou goest, I will go; and where thou lodgest, I will lodge; thy people will be my people, and thy God my God.

CATHERINE DRINKER BOWEN (1897–1973)
American biologist and essayist

Chamber music – a conversation between friends.

ELIZABETH BOWEN (1899–1973)
Anglo-Irish writer
In *The Death of the Heart*

Intimacies between women often go backwards, beginning in revelations and ending up in small talk without loss of esteem.

GENEVIEVE BUJOLD (*b.* 1942)
French-Canadian actress

I would rather be alone than be two people and still alone.

GELETT BURGESS (1866–1951)
American writer

Most women have all women as adversaries; most men have all other men as their allies.

COCO CHANEL (GABRIELLE) (1883–1971)
French conturière

There's nothing worse than solitude, growing old without a shoulder to lean on. Marry, marry – even if he's fat and boring.

JULIA CHILD (*b.* 1912)
American cookery writer and television performer

Remember you're all alone in the kitchen, and no one can see you.

COLETTE (Sidonie-Gabrielle) (1873–1954)
French writer
In L. & M. Cowan's *The Wit of Women*

It is prudent to pour the oil of delicate politeness on the machinery of friendship.

In *Earthly Paradise*

What a delight it is to make friends with someone you have despised!

WILLIAM CONGREVE (1670–1729)
British playwright
In *The Way of the World*

Oh, the pious friendships of the female sex!

BETTE DAVIS (*b.* 1908)
American actress

I am a woman meant for a man, but I never found a man who could compete.

MARLENE DIETRICH (*b.* 1901)
German-born actress

It's the friends you can call up at 4 a.m. that matter.

DIANA DORS (*b.* 1931)
British actress
'Sayings of the Week' (*Observer*, 24 September 1978)

There's nothing more precious in this world than the feeling of being wanted.

GEORGE ELIOT (Marian Evans) (1819–1880)
British novelist
In *Daniel Deronda*

Friendships begin with liking or gratitude – roots that can be pulled up.

A difference of taste in jokes is a great strain on the affections.

In *Middlemarch*

What loneliness is more lonely than distrust?

T. S. ELIOT (1888–1965)
American-born poet
In *The Waste Land*

When lovely woman stoops to folly and
Paces about her room again, alone,
She smoothes her hair with automatic hand
And puts a record on the gramophone.

QUEEN ELIZABETH I (1533–1603)

I would rather be a beggar and single than a queen and married.

EURIPIDES (484–406 BC)
In *Alope*

Woman is woman's natural ally.

MIA FARROW
American actress

If I seem to be running, it's because I'm pursued.

EDNA FERBER (1887–1968)
American writer and playwright
In Robert E. Drennan's *Wit's End*

Being an old maid is like death by drowning, a really delightful sensation after you cease to struggle.

JUDY GARLAND (1922–1969)
American film star

If I'm such a legend, then why am I so lonely? If I'm such a legend, then why do I sit at home for hours staring at the damned telephone, hoping it's out of order, even calling the operator asking her if she's *sure* it's not out of order?

PATRICIA HEARST (*b.* 1954)
American kidnap victim and bank robber

I was coerced.

I died in that fire on 54th Street, but out of the ashes I was reborn.

ERNEST HEMINGWAY (1898–1961)
American novelist
In John Malcolm Brinnin's *The Third Rose*

Gertrude Stein and me are just like brothers . . .

HEDDA HOPPER (1890–1966)
American columnist
In L. & M. Cowan's *The Wit of Women*

Having only friends would be dull anyway – like eating eggs without salt.

GLENDA JACKSON (*b.* 1937)
British actress

I used to believe that anything was better than nothing. Now I know that sometimes nothing is better.

BIANCA JAGGER
Former wife of Mick Jagger

Homosexuals make the best friends because they care about you as a woman and are not jealous. They love you but don't try to screw up your head.

DR SAMUEL JOHNSON (1709–1784)
British writer
In *Rasselas*

The endearing elegance of female friendship.

ERICA JONG (*b.* 1942)
American writer

Solitude is un-American.

JANIS JOPLIN (1943–1970)
American rock singer

On stage I make love to 25,000 people; then I go home alone.

SUZANNE BRITT JORDAN
Quoted in *Newsweek*, 11 June 1979

The perfect mate, despite what *Cosmopolitan* says, does not exist, no matter how many of those tests you take.

HELEN KELLER (1880–1968)
Writer and lecturer (born deaf and blind)
In *My Religion*

What is the use of such terrible diligence as many tire themselves out with, if they always postpone their exchange of smiles with Beauty and Joy to cling to irksome duties and relations?

JACQUELINE KENNEDY ONASSIS (*b.* 1929)
American widow of 35th President of the United States

Now he is a legend when he would have preferred to be a man.

FRAN LEBOWITZ
American journalist
In *Metropolitan Life*

I love sleep because it is both pleasant and safe to use . . . Sleep is death without the responsibility.

ANNE MORROW LINDBERGH (*b.* 1906)
American writer
In *Gift from the Sea*

When one is a stranger to oneself then one is estranged from others too.

In *Locked Rooms and Open Doors*

Men kick friendship around like a football, but it doesn't seem to crack. Women treat it like glass and it goes to pieces.

SOPHIA LOREN (*b.* 1934)
Italian actress

If you have to kiss somebody at 7.00 a.m. (for a film) you'd better be friends.

BETTY MACDONALD (*d.* 1958)
American writer
In *The Egg and I*

In high school and college my sister Mary was very popular

with the boys, but I had braces on my teeth and got high marks.

A woman wants her friend to be perfect. She sets a pattern, usually a reasonable facsimile of herself, lays a friend out on this pattern and worries and prods at any little qualities which do not coincide with her own image.

SHIRLEY MACLAINE (*b.* 1934)
American actress

To the average male there is seemingly nothing so attractive or so challenging as a reasonably good-looking young mother who is married and *alone*.

WILLIAM MCFEE (1881–1966)
British author
In *Harbours of Memory* ('Knights and Turcopoliers')

Wives invariably flourish when deserted; it is the deserting male, the reckless idealist rushing about the world seeking a non-existent felicity, who often ends in disaster.

PHYLLIC MCGINLEY (*b.* 1905)
Canadian writer
In *The Province of the Heart*

Faults shared are comfortable as bedroom slippers and as easy to slip into.

MARYA MANNES (*b.* 1904)
American novelist and poet
In *The Singular Woman*

Self-restraint may be alien to the human temperament, but humanity without restraint will dig its own grave.

CASEY MILLER & KATE SWIFT
In *Words and Women*

Is the sibilant in Ms any more disagreeable to the ear than the hiss in Miss?

LIZA MINNELLI (*b.* 1946)
American actress and singer

Reality is something you rise above.

ETHEL WATTS MUMFORD

God gave us our relatives: thank God we can choose our friends.

DOROTHY PARKER (1893–1967)
American writer and wit
In *The Whistling Girl*

Better be left by twenty dears
Than lie in a loveless bed;
Better a loaf that's wet with tears,
Than cold, unsalted bread.

RUTH PITTER (*b.* 1897)
British poet

The seldom female in a world of males!

DIANE DE POITIERS (1499–1566)

To have a good enemy, choose a friend: he knows where to strike.

THELMA RITTER
American actress
In Universal film *Pillow Talk*

If there's anything worse than a woman living alone, it's a woman saying she likes it.

LINDA RONSTADT (*b.* 1946)
American rock singer

Loneliness is the worst thing about the road . . . it's like travelling through the towns in the Starship Enterprise.

GEORGE BERNARD SHAW (1856–1950)
Irish playwright
In C. St J. Constable's *Ellen Terry and Bernard Shaw: A Correspondence* On Ellen Terry

One may say that her marriages were adventures and her friendships enduring.

PAGE SMITH
In *Daughters of the Promised Land*

After an acquaintance of ten minutes many women will exchange confidences that a man would not reveal to a lifelong friend.

MURIEL SPARK (*b.* 1918)
British novelist

One should only see a psychiatrist out of boredom.

BARBARA WALTERS (*b.* 1931)
American TV presenter
In *How to Talk with Practically Anybody about Practically Anything*

The origin of a modern party is anthropological: humans meet and share food to lower the hostility between them and indicate friendship.

KATHARINE WHITEHORN
British journalist
In *Sunday Best* ('My Best Friend Once Removed')

They are not quite my friends, but I know them better than many who are; they aren't related to me, but they might as well be. They are the close friends of *my* close friends – my friends-in-law.

REV. CORNELIUS WHUR (1782–1853)
In *The Accomplished Female Friend*

But lasting joys the man attend
Who has a polished female friend!

SHELLEY WINTERS (*b.* 1922)
American actress
Quoted in *New York Times*, 18 June 1976

You have a lot of friends who love you dearly and you don't know who they are.

Quoted in *Saturday Evening Post*, 1952

I have bursts of being a lady, but it doesn't last long.

I'm the modern intelligent, independent-type woman. In other words, a girl who can't get a man.

Quoted in Leonard Lyons' column, 11 May 1971

It's so cold here, yesterday I almost got married.

RELIGION

MRS C. F. ALEXANDER (1818–1895)
Hymn writer

All things bright and beautiful,
All creatures great and small,
All things wise and wonderful
The Lord God made them all.

ELIZABETH ARDEN (*circa* 1884–1966)
Canadian beautician

In John Julius Norwich's *A Christmas Cracker*

To be Catholic or Jewish isn't chic. Chic is Episcopalian.

HARRIET AUBER (1773–1862)
Hymn writer

And His that gentle voice we hear,
  Soft as the breath of even,
That checks each fault, that calms each fear,
  And speaks of Heaven.

SIMONE DE BEAUVOIR (*b.* 1908)
French writer

'Sayings of the Week' (*Observer*, 7 January 1979)

I cannot be angry at God, in whom I do not believe.

MARY GARDINER BRAINARD (1837–1905)
In *Not Knowing*

I see not a step before me as I tread on another year;
But I've left the Past in God's keeping – the Future His mercy shall clear;
And what looks dark in the distance, may brighten as I draw near.

ELIZABETH BARRETT BROWNING (1806–1861)
British poet
In *Aurora Leigh*

Some people always sigh in thanking God.

May the good God pardon all good men.

PEARL S. BUCK (1892–1973)
American novelist
In *What America Means to Me*

It may be that religion is dead, and if it is, we had better know it and set ourselves to try to discover other sources of moral strength before it is too late.

CHARLOTTE CAFFEY
American rock singer (*The Go Gos*)

Catholic girls could never consider themselves stars . . . too much fucking guilt.

ALEXIS CARREL (1873–1944)
French biologist

Christianity, above all, has given a clear-cut answer to the demands of the human soul.

LIZZIE YORK CASE (1840–1911)
In *Unbelief*

  There is no unbelief;
Whoever plants a seed beneath the sod
And waits to see it push away the clod,
  He trusts in God.

WILLA CATHER (1873–1947)
American poet
On writing

Religion and art spring from the same root and are close kin. Economics and art are strangers.

ELIZABETH H. J. CLEAVELAND (1824–1911)
In *No Sects in Heaven*

I'm bound for heaven and when I'm there
I shall want my Book of Common Prayer
And though I put on a starry crown,
I should feel quite lost without my gown.

IMOGEN CUNNINGHAM (1833–1976)
American photographer
In *After Ninety*
On being asked her religion by the hospital.

Haven't chosen yet.

EMILY DICKINSON (1830–1886)
American poet

Faith – is the Pierless Bridge
Supporting what We see
Unto the Scene that We do not.

Prayer is the little implement
Through which Men reach
Where Presence – is denied them.

ISADORA DUNCAN (1878–1927)
American dancer
In Lou Tellegen's *Women Have Been Kind*
On herself

Wasn't it Nietzsche who said that he wouldn't believe in a God who could not dance? Neither could I.

MARY BAKER EDDY (1821–1910)
American founder of Christian Science movement

Divine Love always has met and always will meet every human need.

The prayer that reforms the sinner and heals the sick is an absolute faith that all things are possible to God – a spiritual understanding of Him, an unselfed love.

GEORGE ELIOT (Marian Evans) (1819–1880)
British novelist
In *Adam Bede*

We hand folks over to God's mercy, and show none ourselves.

CHARLOTTE ELLIOTT (1789–1871)

Christian, seek not yet repose,
Hear thy guardian angel say,
'Thou art in the midst of foes;
Watch and pray.'

RONALD FIRBANK (1886–1926)
British novelist
In *Valmouth*

'I know of no joy,' she airily began, 'greater than a cool white dress after the sweetness of confession.'

F. SCOTT FITZGERALD (1896–1940)
American writer
In *This Side of Paradise*

She had once been a Catholic, but discovering that priests were infinitely more attentive when she was in process of losing or regaining faith in Mother Church, she maintained an enchanting wavering attitude.

ANTONIA FRASER (*b.* 1932)
British writer
In *My Oxford*

If sexual experiences were theoretically minimal, social expectations were on the contrary great. Once there was a Drag Hunt Ball just outside Oxford, to which I had unaccountably failed to be asked. I asked God to do something about it, and God recklessly killed poor King George VI, as a result of which the Hunt Ball was cancelled.

MARGARET FULLER (1810–1850)
American author and critic
In a letter, 1 March 1838

I myself am more divine than any I see.

WILLA GIBBS (*b.* 1917)
Canadian writer
In *The Dean*

The three kinds of services you generally find in the Episcopal churches. I call them either low-and-lazy, broad-and-hazy, or high-and-crazy.

MRS GREVILLE (*fl.* 1753)
In *Prayer for Indifference*

Nor ease, nor peace, that heart can know,
That like the needle true,
Turns at the touch of joy or woe,
But, turning, trembles too.

MINNIE HASKINS (1875–1957)
British lecturer and poet
In *The Desert*
Quoted by King George VI in his Christmas broadcast, 1939

And I said to the man who stood at the gate of the year: 'Give me a light that I may tread safely into the unknown.' And he replied, 'Go out into the darkness and put your hand into the hand of God. That shall be to you better than light and safer than a known way.'

HELEN KELLER (1880–1968)
Writer and lecturer (born deaf and blind)
In *My Religion*

Science may have found a cure for most evils; but it has found no remedy for the worst of them all – the apathy of human beings.

We cannot freely and wisely choose the right way for ourselves unless we know both good and evil.

In *Let Us Have Faith*

God Himself is not secure, having given man dominion over His works.

Avoiding danger is no safer in the long run than outright exposure. The fearful are caught as often as the bold.

JEAN KERR (*b.* 1923)
American writer
Quoted in *Time*, 14 April 1961

The most important thing about me is that I am a Catholic. It's a superstructure within which you can work, like a sonnet.

KATHRYN KUHLMAN
American writer

You cannot have faith without results any more than you can have motion without movement.

Faith is that quality or power by which the things desired become the things possessed.

GYPSY ROSE LEE (1914–1970)
American stripper

God is love, but get it in writing.

ANNE MORROW LINDBERGH (*b.* 1906)
American writer
In *Dearly Beloved* ('Theodore')

No new sect ever had humour; no disciples either, even the disciples of Christ.

In *Dearly Beloved* ('Locked Rooms and Open Doors')

Damn, damn, damn. I am sick of being this handmaid to the Lord.

MARY WILSON LITTLE
American writer

Men who make no pretensions to being good on one day out of seven are called sinners.

CLARE BOOTHE LUCE (*b.* 1903)
American writer and diplomat

But if God had wanted us to think with our wombs, why did He give us a brain?

MARTIN LUTHER (1483–1546)
German religious reformer

God created Adam lord of all living creatures, but Eve spoiled it all.

MARYA MANNES (*b.* 1904)
American novelist and poet
In *More in Anger*

An American who can make money, invoke God, and be no better than his neighbour, has nothing to fear but truth itself.

DON MARQUIS (1878–1937)
American writer

In all systems of theology the devil figures as a male person. Yet it is women who keep the church going.

MARY MCCARTHY (*b.* 1912)
American writer
Quoted in the *Observer*, 14 October 1979

It really takes a hero to live any kind of spiritual life without religious belief.

And I don't feel the attraction of the Kennedys at all . . . I don't think they are Christians: they may be Catholics but they are not Christians, in my belief anyway.

In *Sheep in Wolves' Clothing*

God is less like air in the lungs, in Graham Greene, than like a depressing smog that hangs over an industrial city . . . He soaks up the smell of his surroundings – bad cooking and mildew and dirty sheets and stale alcohol.

MIGNON MCLAUGHLIN
American writer

I love the idea of God tempering the wind to the shorn lamb, but I'd hate to have to sell it to an American Indian.

On Aimee Semple McPherson (1890–1944)
Anonymous – in *Notable American Women*, vol. 2

The Barnum of religion.

EDNA ST VINCENT MILLAY (1892–1950)
American poet
In *Interim*

Not Truth, but Faith, it is
That keeps the world alive.

NANCY MITFORD (1904–1973)
British writer
In *The Pursuit of Love*

Aunt Sadie . . . so much disliked hearing about health that people often took her for a Christian Scientist, which, indeed, she might have become had she not disliked hearing about religion even more.

DORIS LANGLEY MOORE
British author and costume expert
In *The Vulgar Heart*

The Churches grow old but do not grow up.

MARIANNE MOORE (1887–1972)
American poet
In *Spencer's Ireland*

You're not free
until you've been made captive by
supreme belief.

EDNA O'BRIEN (*b.* 1936)
Irish writer
'Sayings of the Week' (*Observer*)

Ideally I'd like to spend two evenings a week talking to Proust and another conversing to the Holy Ghost.

Quoted in *New York Times*, 11 October 1977

I'm an Irish Catholic and I have a long iceberg of guilt.

PATRICK O'DONOVAN
In *New Republic*, 16 October 1971
On Mother Teresa

She embraces failure. Her work springs from her religion and she will dandle a baby that any fisherman would throw back and rejoice that it has life in it because life itself is divine . . . She in her cheap sari must be the most holy, the most honest, the most real hippie in the world.

DOLLY PARTON (*b.* 1946)
American country singer

I am certainly not a Christian. I will try some of *anything* – I mean I will.

ALICE HEGAN RICE (1870–1942)
In *Mrs Wiggs of the Cabbage Patch*

'Was he a church member?'
'Well no, not exactly,' admitted Mrs Wiggs, reluctantly. 'But he was what you might say a well-wisher.'

BERTRAND RUSSELL (1872–1970)
British philosopher
In *The Basic Writings*, Part II

. . . The nuns who never take a bath without wearing a bathrobe all the time. When asked why, since no man can see them, they reply, 'Oh, but you forget the good God.'

DODIE SMITH (*b.* 1896)
British playwright and novelist
In *I Capture the Castle*

Extreme happiness invites religion almost as much as extreme misery.

PATTI SMITH (*b.* 1946)
American rock singer

I don't want to be like some Hare Krishna weirdo but there are some times when I don't give a fuck about anything else.

SUSAN SONTAG (*b.* 1933)
American essayist
In *Illness as Metaphor*

A large part of the popularity and persuasiveness of psychology comes from its being a sublimated spiritualism: a secular, ostensibly scientific way of affirming the primacy of 'spirit' over matter.

MURIEL SPARK (*b.* 1918)
British novelist
In *The Comforters*

The one certain way for a woman to hold a man is to leave him for religion.

ELIZABETH CADY STANTON (1815–1902)
American suffragette

The Bible and Church have been the greatest stumbling blocks in the way of women's emancipation.

BARONESS MARY STOCKS (1891–1975)
British politician
In *Still More Commonplace*

It is clearly absurd that it should be possible for a woman to qualify as a saint with direct access to the Almighty while she may not qualify as a curate.

LYTTON STRACHEY (1880–1932)
British writer
In *Eminent Victorians*
On Florence Nightingale

Yet her conception of God was certainly not orthodox. She felt towards Him as she might have felt towards a glorified sanitary engineer.

POLY STYRENE (Marion Elliot) (*b.* 1960)
British punk rock singer
After having reverted to her original name and joined the Hare Krishna movement:

Krishna is my manager now.

MOTHER TERESA (*b.* 1910)
Albanian-born nun and Nobel laureate
In Robert Dougall's *Now For the Good News*

Let there be no pride or vanity in the work. The work is God's work, the poor are God's poor. Put yourself completely under the influence of Jesus, so that He may think His thoughts in your mind, do His work through your hands, for you will be all-powerful with Him who strengthens you.

Make sure that you let God's grace work in your souls by accepting whatever He gives you, and giving Him whatever He takes from you.

True holiness consists in doing God's will with a smile.

'Sayings of the Week' (*Observer*, 29 April 1973)

You have a Welfare State. But I have walked your streets at night and gone into your homes and found people dying unloved. Here you have a different kind of poverty. A poverty of spirit, of loneliness and being unwanted. And that is the worst disease in the world: not tuberculosis or leprosy.

SAINT THERESA (1515–1582)

We cannot know whether we love God, although there may

be strong reasons for thinking so, but there can be no doubt about whether we love our neighbour or no.

LILY TOMLIN (*b.* 1939)
American comedienne

Why is it when we talk to God, we're said to be praying – but when God talks to us, we're schizophrenic?

MRS HUMPHRY WARD (1851–1920)
British novelist

Place before your eyes two precepts, and only two. One is Preach the Gospel; and the other is *Put down enthusiasm!*: The Church of England in a nutshell.

SIMONE WEIL (1909–1943)
French writer

We have to believe in a God who is like the true God in everything, except that He does not exist, since we have not reached the point where God exists.

God gives Himself to men as powerful or perfect. It is for them to choose.

EDITH WHARTON (1862–1937)
American novelist

I don't believe in God, but I do believe in His saints.

MARY WOLLSTONECRAFT (1759–1797)
Feminist

I know what you are thinking of, but I have nothing to communicate on the subject of religion.

BARBARA WOODHOUSE
Dog trainer and television personality

I fail utterly to understand religion. I cannot see how God can possibly sort us out when we get to the gates of Heaven or Hell. Surely the sins which we commit every day of our lives, like saying unkind things, or envying those with more possessions than we have, cannot be easily judged against those of, say, child murderers . . . I have a code which I have set myself of trying to say sorry every night before the sun goes down to those I have hurt . . . I don't go to church because I can pray better in the fields.

WORK

ANNABELLA (*circa* 1967)
British rock singer (Bow-Wow-Wow)

I was breathing like having orgasms or something, but the actual thing is that I was supposed to be falling off the Eiffel Tower. That's what I'm actually singing about. Truthfully.

ANONYMOUS AMERICAN LADY
'Sayings of the Week' (*Observer*, 30 April 1972)
When climbing up to the Parthenon

You'd think, with all these tourists about, they would build an elevator.

ELIZABETH GARRETT ANDERSON (1836–1917)
British physician

I was a young woman living at home with nothing to do in what authors call 'comfortable circumstances'. But I was wicked enough not to be comfortable.

MARIAN ANDERSON (*b.* 1902)
American singer

A person has to be busy to stay alive.

ELIZABETH ARDEN (*circa* 1884–1966)
Canadian beautician
In Alfred A. Lewis and Constance Woodworth's *Miss Elizabeth Arden*
To her husband

Dear, never forget one little point. It's my business. You just work here.

HANNAH ARENDT (1906–1975)
German-American political philosopher

There exist labour songs, but no work songs. The songs of the craftsman are social; they are sung after work.

JANE AUSTEN (1775–1817)
British novelist
In *Mansfield Park*

A clergyman has nothing to do but to be slovenly and selfish – read the newspaper, watch the weather, and quarrel with his wife. His curate does all the work and the business of his own life is to dine.

In a letter, 16 December 1816

The little bit of ivory on which I work with so fine a brush as produces little effect after much labour.

MALCOLM BALDRIGE
President, Scoville Manufacturing Co.

A good secretary can save her boss more time in a year than a business jet plane can.

CANDICE BERGEN
American actress
Quoted in *New York Post*, 1967

Hollywood is like Picasso's bathroom.

JUDY BIRMINGHAM
British archaeologist

Archaeology is very much concerned with garbage.

PAULINE BLACK
British rock singer (The Selector)

I am tired of justifying myself. We do what we do, people come to our gigs, they pick up on it, they like it, and it is those people I care about. Journalists can just go take a fuck.

ELIZABETH BOWEN (1899–1973)
Anglo-Irish writer
In *The Death of the Heart*

If you look at life one way, there is always cause for alarm.

KATE BUSH (*b.* 1958)
British singer

When I'm at the piano writing a song, I like to think I'm a man.

JOSEPHINE BUTLER (1828–1906)
British socialist reformer
In E. B. Bell's *Josephine Butler*
On Elizabeth Garrett Anderson

But for Miss Garrett I must say of her that I gained more from her than from any other doctor.

MAMA CASS (Elliott) (1943–1974)
American rock singer

We were the youngest generation of moneyed people and we were just bigger kids about it.

MIGUEL CERVANTES (1547–1616)
Spanish writer
In *Don Quixote*

An honest woman and a broken leg are best at home, and for an honest girl a job of work's her holiday.

SHIRLEY CONRAN
British writer
In *Superwoman* ('The Reason Why')

I make no secret of the fact that I would rather lie on a sofa than sweep beneath it. But you have to be efficient if you're going to be lazy.

Quoted in *Telegraph Sunday Magazine*, 30 October 1977

You cannot have everything and certainly cannot dust everything. To cite Conran's Law of Housework – it expands to fill the time available plus half an hour: so obviously it is never finished . . . Keep housework in its place, which, you will remember, is underfoot.

BETTE DAVIS (*b.* 1908)
American actress
Advice to actress, as quoted by Celeste Holm

Pray to God and say the lines.

MARLENE DIETRICH (*b.* 1901)
German-born actress

I loved them because it is a joy to find thoughts one might have, beautifully expressed . . . by someone . . . wiser than oneself.

BERYL DOWNING
British journalist
Quoted in *The Times*, 1980

Some are born lazy, some have idleness thrust upon them and others spend a great deal of effort creating a careless nonchalance.

SHEENA EASTON
Scottish singer

If I sing a song about my dog dying, it doesn't mean I kill my dog every night before I go on stage.

QUEEN ELIZABETH I (1533–1603)
To Lord William Cecil Burghley – the only person to whom she ever offered a chair in the presence chamber.

We make use of you not for your legs but for your head.

LAURENCE EUSDEN (1688–1730)
British poet

A woman's work, grave sirs, is never done.

MARIANNE FAITHFULL (*b.* 1947)
British actress and rock singer

I wasn't smoking or drinking or taking drugs, and I didn't even sleep around. All I did, from the moment I got up to the minute I fell down in bed, was work – from the age of 17 to 20. Then I found myself living with Jagger and I thought right, I'm now going to start doing a bit of living, and of course, I did with a vengeance.

ELIZABETH FRY (1780–1845)
British Quaker and prison reformer
On criminals

I never refer to their past; we have all sinned and come short.

CELIA GREEN
In *The Decline and Fall of Science* ('Aphorisms')

The way to do research is to attack the facts at the point of greatest astonishment.

LILLIAN HELLMAN (*b.* 1907)
American playwright
In *An Unfinished Woman*

France . . . may be the only country in the world where the rich are sometimes brilliant.

DAME BARBARA HEPWORTH (1903–1975)
British sculptor

It's so natural to work large – it fits one's body.

KATHERINE T. HINKSON (1861–1931)
British poet

It is a horrible demoralising thing to be a lawyer. You look for such low motives in everyone and everything.

WAC BRIGADIER GENERAL ELIZABETH P. HOISINGTON
Quoted in *New York Times*, 20 June 1970

If I had learned to type, I never would have made Brigadier General.

ADA LOUISE HUXTABLE
American writer and critic
Quoted in *New York Times*, 15 February 1976
On Houston, Texas

This city has been an act of real estate, rather than an act of God or man.

CHRISSIE HYNDE
British rock singer (The Pretenders)

It's always been perfectly acceptable for a woman to play the acoustic guitar, but the minute she goes electric, somehow it becomes a sort of mutation. I don't think there is anything strange about it. It's not butch, or macho, it's dead normal to me. I just think of myself as Miss Joe Normal.

MICK JAGGER (*b.* 1943)
British rock singer
Commenting on the launch of 'Apple' by the Beatles

I wouldn't get any satisfaction out of creating a Mary Hopkin.

ANTONY JAY
In *Management and Machiavelli*

The boss's secretary can wield great power, like the king's mistress, without any authority at all.

JANIS JOPLIN (1943–1970)
American rock singer

Getting myself up in the morning – or should I say afternoon, is like picking at a scab.

I'm just gonna keep on rockin' 'cos if I start saving up bits and pieces of me like that, man, there ain't gonna be nothing left for Janis.

You can't rely on inspiration every night.

FLORYNCE KENNEDY (*b.* 1916)
American feminist

There are very few jobs that actually require a penis or a vagina. All other jobs should be open to everybody.

BILLIE JEAN KING (*b.* 1943)
American tennis player

The word is always that amateurs play sport for the love of it. Listen, professionals love it just as much, probably more so. We put our lives on the line for sport.

IRENE KRAMSKY
Quoted in *New York Times*, 29 May 1977

The students are used to being entertained. They are used to the idea that if they are just the slightest bit bored, they can flip the switch and turn the channel.

JUANITE M. KREPS (*b.* 1921)
American economist
Quoted in *Secretary*, June–July 1970

One of the mistakes women have made is to romanticize life in the rose-covered cottage and then, discovering their error, proceed to romanticize life in the working world.

FRAN LEBOWITZ (*circa* 1951)
American journalist

Your child is a writer if . . . you have morning sickness at night because the fetus finds it too distracting to work during the day.

ANNE MORROW LINDBERGH (*b.* 1906)
American writer
In *Hour of Gold, Hour of Lead*

I do not believe that sheer suffering teaches. If suffering alone taught, all the world would be wise.

ANITA LOOS (*b.* 1893)
American novelist

A leader of public thought in Hollywood wouldn't have sufficient mental acumen anywhere else to hold down a place in the bread line.

MARYA MANNES (*b.* 1904)
American novelist and poet
In *More in Anger*

In our society to admit inferiority is to be a fool, and to admit superiority is to be an outcast. Those who are in reality superior in intelligence can be accepted by their fellows only if they pretend they are not.

Quoted in *Life*, 12 June 1964

In the race for money some men may come first, but man comes last.

JAYNE MANSFIELD
American sex symbol

I will do anything to initiate world peace.

MARGARET MEAD (1901–1978)
American anthropologist

I do not believe in using women in combat, because females are too fierce.

HAZEL O'CONNOR (*b.* 1955)
British rock singer

I know I'm an exhibitionist. Maybe that's my art form when you boil it down.

SANDRA DAY O'CONNOR (*b.* 1930)
First woman Justice of the US Supreme Court

About five per cent of judges across the country today are women, and over the next 25 years there will be a vast increase because of the number of women law students today . . . We have a majority of women in the United

States and it is important that they should feel they are involved.

DOROTHY PARKER (1893–1967)
American writer and wit

Hollywood money isn't money. It's congealed snow, melts in your hand, and there you are.

It's not the tragedies that kill us, it's the messes.

DOLLY PARTON (*b.* 1946)
American country singer

I think that women have it made if they know how to go about it. A woman don't have to work, really, if she don't want to and is smart enough to make a man a good wife he's gonna take care of her.

JOAN RIVERS (*b.* 1935)
American comedienne

I hate housework! You make the beds, you do the dishes – and six months later you have to start all over again.

GINGER ROGERS
American film star

The only way to enjoy anything in this life is to earn it first.

ESTHER P. ROTHMAN
In *Troubled Teachers*

Teachers should unmask themselves, admit into consciousness the idea that one does not need to know everything there is to know and one does not have to pretend to know everything there is to know.

MAY SARTON (1488–*circa* 1560)
British 'witch'

It is good for a professional to be reminded that his professionalism is only a husk, that the real person must remain an amateur, a lover of the work.

NINA SIMONE (*b.* 1933)
American jazz singer

I am a genius. I am not your clown. Most of you people out there are crooks. I am an artist not an entertainer . . . and five record companies owe me money.

PATTI SMITH (*b.* 1946)
American rock singer

You take a chance when you put your stakes on somebody else; like a horse race, it often pays, but sooner or later you're gonna be left standing in the rain. Genius is meant to peak and pull out, or to be wiped out permanently.

JANE TRAHEY
In *On Women and Power*

The most likely place to have your idea pocket-picked is at a meeting . . . Here an idea becomes public property the moment it hits the air waves.

KATHARINE WHITEHORN
British journalist
In the *Observer*, 1964

Have you ever taken anything out of the clothes basket because it had become, relatively, the cleaner thing?

In *Sunday Best* (Introduction)
I yield to no one in my admiration for the office as a social centre, but it's no place actually to get any work done.

MARA WOLYNSKI
Quoted in *Newsweek*, 30 August 1976

I've come to see that the real job of the school is to entice the student into the web of knowledge and then, if he's not enticed, to drag him in.

SUCCESS AND FAILURE

CINDY ADAMS

Success has made failures of many men.

FRED ALLEN (1894–1956)
American actor

Success is like dealing with your kid or teaching your wife to drive. Sooner or later you'll end up in the police station.

ELIZABETH ARDEN (*circa* 1884–1966)
Canadian beautician

The cosmetics industry is the nastiest business in the world.

LADY NANCY ASTOR (1879–1964)
First woman to sit in the House of Commons

The only thing I like about rich people is their money.

JIM BACKUS (*b.* 1913)
American actor

Many a man owes his success to his first wife, and his second wife to his success.

JOAN BAEZ (*b.* 1941)
American folk singer

I don't want to be the world's oldest living folk singer.

LESTER BANGS

Having Linda McCartney on stage in a multi-million dollar tour is like hiring a good black construction worker to edit the *New York Times*.

BRIGITTE BARDOT (*b.* 1934)
French actress

I'm a woman who has undoubtedly made a success of her career, but not of her private life. Perhaps in five years I'll be able to live like everyone else . . . I'll no longer be a beautiful object, but a human being.

PAT BENATAR
American rock singer

I'm the pretty-girl-who-can-sing stereotype. I never knew I was gonna get it this bad. All of a sudden you realize, 'Shit, people are looking at my crotch. This is embarrassing.'

RUTH BENEDICT (1887–1948)
American anthropologist
In M. Mead's *An Anthropologist at Work*

The trouble is not that we are never happy – it is that happiness is so episodical.

INGRID BENGIS (*b.* 1944)
American feminist

The real trap of fame is its irresistibility.

INGRID BERGMAN (1915–1982)
Swedish actress

Happiness is good health and a bad memory.

CLAIRE BLOOM (*b.* 1931)
British actress

I like to work in Hollywood but I don't like to live there. I'm too young to die.

AIMÉE BUCHANAN

Too often a sense of loyalty depends on admiration, and if we can't admire it is difficult to be loyal.

ABIGAIL VAN BUREN (*b.* 1918)
American writer and journalist

If you want a place in the sun you've got to put up with a few blisters.

HORTENSE CALISHER (*b.* 1911)
American novelist

An artist is born kneeling; he fights to stand. A critic, by nature of the judgement seat, is born sitting.

MARIA CALLAS (1923–1977)
In *Kenneth Harris Talking to: 'Maria Callas'*

That is the difference between good teachers and great teachers: good teachers make the best of a pupil's means: great teachers foresee a pupil's ends.

ROY CAR
Music journalist
In *New Musical Express*

In America Debbie Harry is the girl next door, only if you live in a bad neighbourhood.

COCO CHANEL (Gabrielle) (1883–1971)
French couturière
In M. Haedrich's *Coco Chanel – Her Life, Her Secrets*

In order to be irreplaceable one must always be different.

CAROL CHANNING (*b.* 1921)
American actress

Laughter is much more important than applause. Applause is almost a duty. Laughter is a reward.

AGATHA CHRISTIE (1891–1976)
British thriller writer
In *Sparkling Cyanide*

The happy people are failures because they are on such good terms with themselves that they don't give a damn.

BEATRICE COLEN
Quoted in *Image*, January 1974

The failure is to be forty and not to have tried.

COLETTE (Sidonie-Gabrielle) (1873–1954)
French writer

To talk to a child, to fascinate him, is much more difficult than to win an electoral victory. But it is also more rewarding.

JILLY COOPER (*b.* 1937)
British writer
In Neil Mackwood's *In and Out: Debrett 1980/81*

Life is happier if it is full of pretty people.

EMILY DICKINSON (1830–1886)
American poet

Success is counted sweetest
By those who ne'er succeed.

PHIL DONAHUE
Quoted in *Newsweek*, 13 March 1978

Women are smarter then men because they listen.

MARGARET DRABBLE (*b.* 1939)
British novelist
In L. & M. Cowan's *The Wit of Women*

Nothing succeeds, they say, like success. And certainly nothing fails like failure.

MARIANNE FAITHFULL (*b.* 1947)
British actress and rock singer

I've been living on royalties from *Sister Morphine* for ten years. Don't tell me drugs don't pay.

You've got to be awfully careful what you say about heroin: you mustn't give anybody the impression it's a good thing. It's totally ghastly.

WILLIAM FAULKNER (1879–1962)
American novelist

Success is feminine and like a woman; if you cringe before her, she will override you. So the way to treat her is to show her the back of your hand. Then maybe she will do the crawling.

FARAH FAWCETT (*b.* 1948)
American actress

God made men stronger but not necessarily more intelligent. He gave women intuition and femininity. And, used properly, that combination easily jumbles the brain of any man I've ever met.

MARGOT FONTEYN (*b.* 1919)
British ballerina

Great artists are people who find the way to be themselves in their art.

BETTY FORD
Wife of former US President

A liberated woman is one who feels confident in herself, and is happy in what she is doing. She is a person who has a sense of self . . . It all comes down to freedom of choice.

ELLEN FRANKFORT

Choice has always been a privilege of those who could afford to pay for it.

MARGARET FULLER (OSSOLI) (1810–1850)
Quoted in *New York Tribune*, 1833

Truth is the nursing mother of genius. No man can be absolutely true to himself, eschewing cant, compromise, servile imitation, and complaisance, without becoming original for there is in every creature a fountain of life which, if not choked back by stones and other dead rubbish, will create a fresh atmosphere, and bring to life fresh beauty.

In *Diary*

Genius will live and thrive without training, but it does not the less reward the watering-pot and pruning-knife.

JUDY GARLAND (1922–1969)
American actress

In the silence of night I have often wished for just a few words of love from one man, rather than the applause of thousands of people.

J. PAUL GETTY (1892–1976)
American millionaire
In *As I See It*
On his wives

Each [of them] was jealous and resentful of my preoccupation with business. Yet none showed any visible aversion to sharing in the proceeds.

HERMIONE GINGOLD (*b.* 1897)
British actress

I got all the schooling any actress needs. That is, I learned to write enough to sign contracts.

LILLIAN GISH (*b.* 1896)
American actress

A happy life is one spent in learning, earning and yearning.

EMMA GOLDMAN (1869–1940)
American anarchist

Idealists . . . foolish enough to throw caution to the winds . . . have advanced mankind and have enriched the world.

RUTH GORDON (*b.* 1896)
American actress

I think there is one smashing rule: Never face the facts.

KATHERINE GRAHAM (*b.* 1917)
American newspaper executive

I always thought if you worked hard enough and tried hard enough, things would work out. I was wrong.

MARGARET CASE HARRIMAN

Money is what you'd get on beautifully without if only other people weren't so crazy about it.

HELEN HAYES (*b.* 1900)
American actress
In Roy Newquist's *Showcase*

Every human being on this earth is born with a tragedy, and it isn't original sin. He's born with the tragedy that he has to grow up . . . a lot of people don't have the courage to do it.

LILLIAN HELLMAN (*b.* 1909)
American playwright

Nobody outside of a baby carriage or a judge's chamber can believe in an unprejudiced point of view.

Success and failure are not true opposites and they're not even in the same class; they're not even a couch and a chair.

It doesn't pay well to fight for what we believe in.

KATHARINE HEPBURN (*b.* 1909)
American film actress

Life is to be lived. If you have to support yourself, you had bloody well better find some way that is going to be interesting. And you don't do that by sitting around wondering about yourself.

What the hell – you might be right, you might be wrong – but don't just *avoid*.

BILLIE HOLIDAY (1915–1959)
American blues singer

I'm always making a comeback but nobody ever tells me where I've been.

I had to be darkened down so that the show could go in dynamic-arsed Detroit. It's like they say, there's no damn business like show business. You had to smile to keep from throwing up.

HEDDA HOPPER (1890–1966)
American gossip columnist

Two of the cruellest, most primitive punishments our town deals out to those who fall from favour are the empty mailbox and the silent telephone.

At one time I thought he wanted to be an actor. He had certain qualifications, including no money and a total lack of responsibility.

ELIZABETH JANE HOWARD (*b.* 1923)
British writer
Quoted in *The Listener*, 1978

The capacity for pleasure is an art; and relatively few people are good at it over a wide range.

BIANCA JAGGER
Former wife of Mick Jagger

People think I live a dissipated life. That is not true. Drugs are a cheat. I can see it right away in the colour of the skin, in the quality of the hair, the nails – the brilliance of the eyes. Look at me – do I look like a heroin addict?

GRACE JONES
West Indian-born rock singer

Men are afraid of me. They're scared stiff. They take one look at me and run in the opposite direction. I have to grab them, throw them down and smack them a couple of times. But some guys realize there is a whole other side to me – sort of a little girl side.

ERICA JONG (*b.* 1942)
American writer

No scared housewife. I was flying.

JANIS JOPLIN (1943–70)
American rock singer

At my concerts, most of the chicks are looking for liberation. They think I'm going to show them how to do it.

HELEN KELLER (1880–1968)
Writer and lecturer (born deaf and blind)

One can never consent to creep when one feels an impulse to soar.

BILLIE JEAN KING (*b.* 1943)
American tennis player
Quoted in *New York Times*, 14 January 1976

If you're small, you better be a winner. (Billie Jean is 5′ 4½″.)

I'm not radical – I'm just aware. I've come a long way, baby.

DR GRAYSON KIRK (*b.* 1903)
American academic

It would be preposterously naïve to suggest that a B.A. can be made as attractive to girls as a marriage licence.

OLGA KORBUT (*b.* 1955)
Russian gymnast

I am not interested in medals or titles. I don't need them. I need the love of the public and I fight for it.

MICHAEL KORDA (*b.* 1933)
American writer

Men are never so tired and harassed as when they have to deal with a woman who wants a raise.

ANN LANDERS (*b.* 1918)
American journalist

Opportunities are usually diguised as hard work, so most people don't recognize them.

HELEN LAWRENSON
American journalist
Quoted in *Esquire*, 1971

If a woman is sufficiently ambitious, determined *and* gifted – there is practically nothing she can't do.

BEATRICE LILLIE (Lady Peel) (*b.* 1894)
Canadian actress

'What beautiful pearls, Beatrice. Are they real?' asked a titled lady at a reception.

'Of course,' Miss Lillie replied.

But to make sure, the woman took hold of the string and bit one of the pearls.

'They're not,' she jeered. 'They're cultured.'

'And how could you know, Duchess, with false teeth?' came the reply.

KAY LYONS

Yesterday is a cancelled cheque; tomorrow is a promissory note; today is the only cash you have – so spend it wisely.

MARYA MANNES (*b.* 1904)
American novelist and poet

The suppression of civil liberties is to many less a matter for horror than the curtailment of the freedom to profit.

ELSA MAXWELL (1883–1963)
American socialite

Keep your talent in the dark and you'll never be insulted.

MARY McCOY

The trouble with being a breadwinner nowadays is that the Government is in for such a big slice.

PHYLLIS McGINLEY (*b.* 1905)
Canadian writer
In *The Province of the Heart*

Nothing fails like success; nothing is so defeated as yesterday's triumphant cause.

MIGNON McLAUGHLIN
American writer

There are so many things that we wish we had done yesterday, so few that we feel like doing today.

There are a handful of people whom money won't spoil, and we count ourselves among them.

We'd all like a reputation for generosity and we'd all like to buy it cheap.

MERLE L. MEACHAM

Xerox: A trademark for a photocopying device that can make rapid reproductions of human error, perfectly.

GRANDMA MOSES (Anna Mary Robertson) (1860–1961)
American painter

A primitive artist is an amateur whose work sells.

HAZEL O'CONNOR (*b.* 1955)
British rock singer

You write your name on infinity or you blow it. I'm writing my name on infinity. I've decided. And He knows.

I don't expect to move the world, you know. Just 90 per cent of it.

I eat the same, the only measure of my success is now I always have champagne in the fridge.

YOKO ONO (*b.* 1933)
Japanese-born artist

If the butterflies in your stomach die, send yellow death announcements to your friends.

DOROTHY PARKER (1893–1967)
American writer and wit

I'm never going to be famous. My name will never be writ large on the roster of Those Who Do Things. I don't do anything. Not one single thing. I used to bite my nails, but I don't even do that any more.

DOLLY PARTON (*b.* 1946)
American country singer

I had a rough time in school because I was the most popular girl in the wrong way . . . I had a lot of stories told on me, a lot of lies, just because I looked the way I did. I was always big in the boobs, small in the waist and big in the butt. I just grew up that way, and I had that foxy personality too.

LUCINDA PRIOR-PALMER
British horsewoman
Quoted in *The Guardian*, 1976

I mean, fame's quite fun and all that, but as soon as anything goes wrong or you make a big bog of something, everyone knows about it and that does taint it a bit.

IRENE PETER

Anyone who thinks there's safety in numbers hasn't looked in the stock market pages.

LETTY COTTIN POGREBIN (*b.* 1939)
American writer

Boys don't make passes at female smart-asses.

MARGARET PYKE
Chairman, British Family Planning Association, 1962

In a final estimate Marie Stopes may well prove to have been one of the most important and outstanding influences of the twentieth century – a judgement with which, one feels sure, she would be in complete agreement.

MARY QUANT (*b.* 1934)
British fashion designer

I think I was born never wanting to grow up.

ESTELLE RAMEY

President, Association of Women in Science

We will have equality when a female schlemiel moves ahead as fast as a male schlemiel.

HELEN REDDY

American singer

From 'I am woman'

If I have to, I can do anything, I am strong; I am invincible; I am woman.

VANESSA REDGRAVE (*b.* 1937)

British actress

In D. Bailey's *Goodbye Baby and Amen*

Integrity is so perishable in the summer months of success.

GINGER ROGERS

American film star

Hollywood is like an empty wastebasket.

ELEANOR ROOSEVELT (1884–1962)

Wife of 32nd President of the United States

I believe that anyone can conquer fear by doing the things he fears to do, provided he keeps doing them until he gets a record of successful experiences behind him.

I think somehow, we learn who we really are and then live with that decision.

DIANA ROSS (*b.* 1944)
American singer

Either black people end up being the best in sports, or else it's show business. You know, we all got rhythm.

JUDITH ROSSNER
American novelist
In *Attachments*, 1977

Some people spend their lives failing and never notice.

ROSALIND RUSSELL (1911–1976)
American actress

Success is a public affair. Failure is a private funeral.

ADELA ROGERS ST JOHN (*b.* 1894)
American writer

God made man, and then said I can do better than that and made woman.

SERVICES AND INDUSTRY, 1966

Nothing so stirs a man's conscience or excites his curiosity as a woman's complete silence.

WILLIAM SHAKESPEARE (1564–1616)
British playwright
In *Henry VI: Part I*

She's beautiful and therefore to be wooed; She is a woman, therefore to be won.

MARLENA SHAW
American singer

Success means only being exposed to more people.

MOTHER SHIPTON (mid-16th century)
English prophetess

Carriages without horses shall go
And accidents fill the world with woe.

Around the world thoughts shall fly
In the twinkling of an eye.

BEVERLY SILLS (*b.* 1929)
American singer and opera director

I'm the Beatles of the opera.

NANCY SINATRA (*b.* 1940)
American actress

It's a hectic, crazy life. You're not like a shoe salesman, who can get rid of his wares. You're stuck with a product – yourself.

GRACE SLICK (*b.* 1939)
American rock singer

With a person who is an alcoholic as I am, you don't ever have one or two drinks. It doesn't work that way. I've never had two drinks in my life.

LIZ SMITH

A true celebrity was someone identifiable by name only.

PATTI SMITH (*b.* 1946)
American rock singer
On her brother, Todd

He's, like, Leonardo da Vinci. Only in his own stuff. My whole family is, like, fulla da Vincis. He can do anything great. He's a great butcher.

SUSAN SONTAG (*b.* 1933)
American essayist

The purpose of art is always, ultimately, to give pleasure – though our sensibilities may take time to catch up with the forms of pleasure that art in a given time may offer.

GERTRUDE STEIN (1974–1946)
American writer

Money is always there but the pockets change; it is not in the same pockets after a change, and that is all there is to say about money.

JAMES STEWART (*b.* 1908)
American actor

Behind every successful man you'll find a woman who has nothing to wear.

DR MARIE STOPES (1880–1958)
British birth control pioneer

In a marginal scribble in a Catholic Truth Society pamphlet, 1919.

I will be canonized in 200 years time.

LYTTON STRACHEY (1880–1932)
British writer
In *Queen Victoria*, 1921

If Victoria had died in the early seventies, there can be little doubt that the voice of the world would have pronounced her a failure.

BARBRA STREISAND (*b.* 1942)
American actress and singer

Success to me is having ten honeydew melons and eating only the top half of each one.

JACQUELINE SUSANN (1921–1974)
American writer

Money is applause.

ELIZABETH TAYLOR (*b.* 1932)
British-born actress

There's no deodorant like success.

DAME ELLEN TERRY (1847–1928)
British actress

Security is mortal's chiefest enemy.

LILY TOMLIN (*b.* 1939)
American comedienne

The trouble with the rat race is that even if you win, you're still a rat!

Sometimes I worry about being a success in a mediocre world.

SOPHIE TUCKER (1884–1960)
American singer

Success in show business depends on your ability to make and keep friends.

LANA TURNER (*b.* 1920)
American actress

A successful man is one who makes more money than his wife can spend.
A successful woman is one who can find such a man.

QUEEN VICTORIA (1819–1901)
To A. J. Balfour, December 1899

We are not interested in the possibilities of defeat.

COMTESSE DE VOIGRAND

There are poor men in this country who cannot be bought: the day I found that out, I sent my gold abroad.

VIRGINIA WADE (*b.* 1945)
British tennis player

Winners aren't popular. Losers often are.

BARBARA WALTERS (*b.* 1931)
American television presenter

I didn't get ahead by sleeping with people. Girls, take heart!

CHARLES DUDLEY WARNER (1829–1900)

Women are not so sentimental as men, and are not so easily touched with the unspoken poetry of nature; being less poetical, and having less imagination, they are more fitted for practical affairs, and would make less failures in business.

SIMONE WEIL (1909–1943)
French writer

The distance between the necessary and the good is the distance between the creature and the creator.

MAE WEST (1892–1980)
American film star

She's the kind of girl who climbed the ladder of success, wrong by wrong.

MARY WIGMAN

Strong and convincing art has never arisen from theories.

ELLA WHEELER WILCOX (1855–1919)
American writer
In *To Lift or to Lean*

The two kinds of people on earth that I mean
Are the people who lift and the people who lean.

OSCAR WILDE (1854–1900)
Irish writer

One must have a heart of stone to read of the death of Little Nell without laughing.

NANCY WILDON
American rock singer (Heart)

We could try inviting whole audiences out to dinner.

SHELLEY WINTERS (*b.* 1922)
American actress

Stardom can be very destructive – particularly if you believe in it.

VIRGINIA WOOLF (1882–1941)
British writer

One likes people much better when they're battered down by a prodigious siege of misfortune than when they triumph.

MARGUERITE YOURCENAR (*b.* 1903)
French writer

All happiness is innocence.